AMERICAN DWIGHT K. NELSON
APOCALYPSE

Pacific Press®
Publishing Association
Nampa, Idaho | www.pacificpress.com

Cover design by Gerald Lee Monks
Cover design resources
    Flag: iStockphoto.com | RomoloTavani
    Crowd: iStockphoto.com | Nosyrevy
    Statue: iStockphoto.com | Vladone
Inside design by Aaron Troia

The author assumes full responsibility for the accuracy of all facts and quotations as cited in this book.

Unless otherwise noted, all Scripture quotations are from THE HOLY BIBLE, NEW INTERNATIONAL VERSION®. Copyright © 1973, 1978, 1984, 2011 by Biblica, Inc.® Used by permission. All rights reserved worldwide.

Scripture quotations marked KJV are from the King James Version.

Scripture quotations marked NKJV are from the New King James Version®. Copyright © 1982 by Thomas Nelson. Used by permission. All rights reserved.

Scripture quotations marked NRSV are from the New Revised Standard Version of the Bible, copyright © 1989 by the Division of Christian Education of the National Council of the Churches of Christ in the USA. Used by permission. All rights reserved.

Purchase additional copies of this book by calling toll-free 1–800–765–6955 or by visiting AdventistBookCenter.com.

Library of Congress Cataloging-in-Publication Data

Names: Nelson, Dwight K., author.
Title: American apocalypse / Dwight K. Nelson.
Description: Nampa, Idaho : Pacific Press Publishing Association, [2021] | Summary: "A biblical analysis of today's America in the stream of prophetic history"—Provided by publisher.
Identifiers: LCCN 2021025554 (print) | LCCN 2021025555 (ebook) | ISBN 9780816367702 | ISBN 9780816367719 (ebook)
Subjects: LCSH: Bible. Revelation—Criticism, interpretation, etc. | Bible—Prophecies—United States. | Christianity—United States. | United States—Church history. | General Conference of Seventh-day Adventists—Doctrines.
Classification: LCC BS2825.52 .N45 2021 (print) | LCC BS2825.52 (ebook) | DDC 228/.06—dc23
LC record available at https://lccn.loc.gov/2021025554
LC ebook record available at https://lccn.loc.gov/2021025555

July 2021

To my favorite granddaughters,

Ella and Isabelle (and their little sister soon to be born)—

We will tell the next generation [your parents]

the praiseworthy deeds of the LORD [your Savior], . . .

so the next generation [you] would know them,

even the children yet to be born [your sister].

—Psalm 78:4, 6

CONTENTS

"The Lord has done more for the United States than for any other country upon which the sun shines."

And it is into this tension—that America is exceptional but not superior—this book must step.

PREFACE FROM CAPITOL HILL:
YOU CAN GET THERE FROM HERE

Who will forget the shocking images we witnessed live on our screens that Wednesday afternoon, January 6, 2021? I was in a meeting in my church office with one of our worship leaders when my cell phone began to vibrate incessantly with incoming text messages. I tried (you know the drill) to concentrate on our conversation while surreptitiously (I'm sure it was obvious) sliding the phone closer to me so I could finally make out a text message: "Are you watching this?" Watching what? The attached picture was too small.

As soon as the meeting ended, I grabbed the phone and clicked on the texted image. I couldn't believe what I saw. So I flipped open my laptop and, sure enough—live on my screen in slow-motion meltdown—a rampaging mob of Americans crashing the barricades, scaling the walls, smashing the windows and doors of the United States Capitol building. Unfathomable!

So here I am, this American kid, born in Tokyo, Japan. And whenever my missionary parents would come home on "furlough," we would head to Washington, DC, to visit my grandparents, who lived in the suburbs. And every time I walked into that iconic, massive white-marbled edifice, I confess it felt like I was in church, in a vaulted cathedral where "whispers only" is the rule, where the famous and mighty of history—my boyhood heroes—once echoed down these halls.

So you will forgive my emotions that Wednesday afternoon, as I stared with anger and fear, my eyes welling with sadness, as this pantheon of democracy was overrun by a crush of frenzied Americans incited to insurrection. And the rest is history—a tragic and troubling history now—for every American, no matter how you voted or where you are from.

Perhaps this history is but the dire fruit of what the ancient prophet Hosea warned: "They sow the wind and reap the whirlwind" (Hosea 8:7).

The on-camera, nine-minute suffocation of George Floyd beneath the knee of a police officer in Minneapolis in the summer of 2020 blew a stiff wind across this "O beautiful for spacious skies" [1] America, homeland to nearly one-third of a billion people.

And the subsequent erupting Black Lives Matter protests that shut down swaths of Seattle, Portland, and Washington, DC, all of it in the midst of a crippling pandemic that has yet to vacate the premises, only sowed an even stiffer wind "above the fruited plain."

"Sow the wind, reap the whirlwind." Was the whirlwind this nation reaped the fractured electoral process in the autumn that split a nation already divided? Or was the storming of Capitol Hill by those trespassing revolutionaries that left five Americans dead but the last straw before the whirlwind?

In his book *The Soul of America: The Battle for Our Better Angels*, the Pulitzer Prize–winning biographer and historian Jon Meacham asserts: "America has been defined by a sense of its own exceptionalism—an undertaking of destiny that has also been tempered by an appreciation of the tragic nature of life. . . . We try; we fail; but we must try again, and again, and again, for only in trial is progress possible." [2]

I suppose we get the "try and fail" part. Whether you are an American or not, it is a life skill we have all honed. So "try and fail" hardly makes any of us exceptional. Then why bring up "American exceptionalism" at all? After all, the case can surely be made that every country in its own uniqueness is an example of exceptionalism—this notion that "a species, country, society, institution, movement, individual, or time period is 'exceptional' (i.e., unusual or extraordinary) . . . [with] the implication, whether or not specified, that the referent is superior in some way." [3]

Is America superior to the rest of the world? I do not believe it is. Although scribbled on the top of the page that contains Revelation 13 in my Bible are these words: "The Lord has done more for the United States than for any other country upon which the sun shines." [4]

And it is into this tension—that America is exceptional but not superior—this book must step. In these pages, I invite you to examine with me a troubling piece of the Apocalypse. It is a prophetic word. And there are many, schooled and studied, who conclude that this apocalyptic scenario is a cryptic depiction of American exceptionalism turned tragic. Just how tragic we will see as we lay down the saga of this nation beside the unblinking eye of divine prophecy.

Is there hope for America? More than you can imagine. The COVID-19 pandemic that still ravages this land—the racial, economic, political, and social fractures that divide us—all of this notwithstanding, I believe the greatest days (though not necessarily the best) are yet ahead. And if the motto pressed onto the coinage and printed on the currency of this nation is to be believed, then In God We Trust may yet be the deliverance of our national soul and the salvation of a history still to be written.

American Apocalypse is an invitation to both pray for that salvation and work for that deliverance. For it is Americans more than America the "better angels" seek to save. As Meacham concludes: "There is, in fact, no struggle more important, and none nobler, than the one we wage in the service of those better angels who, however besieged, are always ready for battle."[5]

A battle, I might add, of unimagined cosmic consequences. A battle in which you and I are engaged, whether we want to be or not. To that battle for America we must now turn. With hope.

Dwight K. Nelson
Pioneer Memorial Church
on the campus of Andrews University

---

1. Katharine Lee Bates, "America the Beautiful" (1893).

2. Jon Meacham, *The Soul of America: The Battle for Our Better Angels* (New York: Random House, 2018), 10.

3. Wikipedia, s.v. "Exceptionalism," last modified May 6, 2021, https://en.wikipedia.org/wiki/Exceptionalism.

4. Ellen G. White, *Maranatha* (Washington, DC: Review and Herald®, 1976), 193.

5. Meacham, *The Soul of America*, 272.

Clearly, the Apocalypse is *not* the revelation of the church or the revelation of Rome or the revelation of America, *not* even the revealing of the antichrist and the demonic endgame. First and foremost, the book that undergirds these pages is "the revelation of Jesus Christ."

DOOMSCROLLING THE FUTURE

Americans have discovered a new pastime. You may be an expert at it. Scroll, click, skim. Scroll, click, skim. It's how everybody reads their news feeds anymore. Ever watch a young Gen Zer speed through the eye-and-thumb scroll-click-skim routine? Like lightning. I get worn out just watching! The truth is we all do it so well they have coined a psychosocial term for it.

Sophie Bushwick, an associate editor covering technology at *Scientific American*, defines the new word: "Reading through their social media feeds, Americans are likely to encounter anguished accounts of political turmoil, the coronavirus pandemic and continued fallout from cyber-attacks, among other less-than-cheerful topics. And yet, many can't stop scrolling even more, perhaps hoping to distract themselves from thinking too hard about any one of these ongoing problems. The practice has earned a suitably apocalyptic nickname: doomscrolling."[1]

Did you catch that—"a suitably apocalyptic nickname"? Because, have you noticed, apocalyptic is how life around the planet feels these days? Nobody is sure anymore. Which explains why our thumbs and minds scroll through our news feeds with the fleeting hope that perhaps today we'll find the elusive key or story that will unlock this apocalyptic riddle we're living, or at least explain the numinous foreboding that refuses to lift from our anxious minds. Doomscrolling.

You can even do it with the Apocalypse, the Bible's last book, regarded by many as the ultimate doomsday or doomscrolling literature. But to leap to that assumption is to simply jump to conclusions and risk missing the passionate, dramatic heart and soul of Revelation.

So let's insert two critical baselines, two nonnegotiables that must by necessity inform the very necessary doomscrolling we will have to engage in to confront the apocalyptic future of America.

Baseline no. 1—"The revelation from Jesus Christ, which God gave him to show his servants what must soon take place" (Revelation 1:1).
There is no equivocation in the first line of the Apocalypse. *Apokalupsis Iesou Christou* is the opening salvo of the document the elderly John scribbled onto parchment from his Patmos promontory overlooking the windswept Aegean Sea. The aged prisoner is no longer the "John Boy" of Jesus' twelve disciples. As the last surviving apostle, John is affectionately known to his parishioners in the late first-century Christian community as the Elder (*shepherd* or *pastor*).[2] But now, the elderly man is incarcerated on that rocky Roman penal colony because of his unshakable faith in his Master and Savior. Tradition records that the emperor Domitian banished John to Patmos after unsuccessfully attempting to execute him in a cauldron of boiling oil. Such was his unrelenting trust in Jesus.

When John pens the words "the revelation *of* Jesus Christ," the phrase can be accurately rendered in English either "the revelation *from* Jesus Christ" or "the revelation *about* Jesus Christ."

Ranko Stefanovic notes: "In a sense, both meanings are implied here. While the revelation came from God through Jesus Christ, who communicated it to John through an angel (Rev. 1:1; cf. 22:16), the rest of the book testifies that Jesus is the main subject of its contents. He is 'the Alpha and the Omega' (that is, the A to Z) of the book's content, 'the beginning and the end' (21:6; 22:13), and 'the first and the last' (1:17; 22:13). *The book begins and concludes with Jesus.*"[3]

We forget that reality, to our loss. Clearly, the Apocalypse is *not* the revelation of the church or the revelation of Rome or the revelation of America, *not* even the revealing of the antichrist and the demonic endgame. First and foremost, the book that undergirds these pages is "the revelation of Jesus Christ." He is its Hero, the theme of its jubilant songs, the Victor of its crimson and cosmic battles, some yet to be fought. As Elizabeth Talbot repeatedly and rightfully exclaims, "Jesus wins!"[4]

"The revelation of Jesus Christ" signals the reader that whatever we may discover in this book, whatever prophecy we may explore, whatever prediction we may examine together, whatever pronouncements we may overhear, whatever this book may be about, it is firstly and supremely a revelation of Jesus to your life right now, "a unique portrayal of Christ not found elsewhere in the Scriptures."[5]

Some have suggested it is an urban legend, this story of the New Mexico gem dealer Roy Whetstine. Walking through the exhibits of an amateur rock collectors' convention, Whetstine stopped by the table of a rock hound from Idaho. In a Tupperware bowl of discarded stones selling for $15 each, he found a dull, egg-shaped rock. Carefully examining it, Whetstine turned to the amateur collector and asked, "You want $15 for *this*?" The collector snatched the stone from Whetstine, looked it over, then shook his head. "No, you can have it for $10." And with that $10 purchase, Whetstine walked away with the world's largest star sapphire, an estimated value of $1.7 million.

Urban legend or not, the point is inescapable. Beware of overlooking the familiar when searching for the exotic. The study of Revelation is not a search for the exotic. Its carefully crafted and positioned opening line—"the revelation of Jesus Christ"—is the priceless exhibit it offers. It is quite literally the revealing of the Lord Jesus Christ. He is not a hidden Where's Waldo? figure. He is the towering God-man whose incarnation story has already been told in the elderly John's fourth gospel. John now presents Him once again to the reader as the *sine qua non* of all divine revelation.

In the words of the American writer Ellen White: "Were thousands of the most gifted men to devote their whole time to setting forth Jesus always before us, studying how they might portray His matchless charms, they would never exhaust the subject."[6]

Baseline no. 1 for our doomscrolling the future—"the revelation of Jesus Christ."

Baseline no. 2—"And there was war in heaven" (Revelation 12:7, KJV).

No other book of Scripture more graphically discloses the internecine war instigated by the fallen rebel angel of heaven eons ago than the Apocalypse (with perhaps the book of Job a runner-up). If Jesus is the *subject* of the Apocalypse (baseline no. 1), His crushing defeat of Satan is the *focus* of the Apocalypse (baseline no. 2). Every reader who picks up the book of Revelation is already deeply and existentially engaged in the raging warfare the Apocalypse dramatically exposes. No wonder the first of seven blessings pronounced in Revelation declares: "Blessed is the one who reads aloud the words of this prophecy, and blessed are those who hear it and take to heart what is written in it, because the time is near" (Revelation 1:3).

But what is so blessed about discovering that "there was war in heaven"? This can hardly be a mythological Luke Skywalker and Darth Vader lightsaber fight to the death, can it? The cryptic language John chooses in this second critical baseline is a vital clue. The Greek word for "war" is *polemos*, from whence come our English words *polemics* and *polemical*—two words that strongly hint not of hand-to-hand combat but rather mind-to-mind, ideology-versus-ideology warfare, a cosmic war of words, a deadly battle of competing allegiances.

As Sigve Tonstad notes: " 'War' (*polemos*) is one of the most important words in the book, as a noun (9:7, 9; 12:7, 17; 13:7; 16:14; 19:19; 20:8) or as a verb (*polemeo*) with the meaning 'to wage war' (12:7; 13:4; 17:14; 19:11). No sentence is more representative than the statement, '*There was war . . .*' (12:7). 'War' has a military connotation; 'polemics' is a form of disagreement playing out in the realm of opinion and argument. This notion fits the conflict in Revelation better than an outright matchup of conflicting parties in the realm of power."[7]

> Revelation's prophecies, with their more than mythological staging, turn out to be stunning and graphic depictions of the desperate war still raging between the forces of light and darkness on this planetary battlefield in this very moment of time, of history.

Thus, Revelation's prophecies, with their more than mythological staging, turn out to be stunning and graphic depictions of the desperate war still raging between the forces of light and darkness on this planetary battlefield in this very moment of time, of history.

These words may read like a dark story. But be warned. They are the tale of a reality we now live:

> Then war broke out in heaven. Michael and his angels fought against the dragon, and the dragon and his angels fought back. But he was not strong enough, and they lost their place in heaven. The great dragon was hurled down—that ancient serpent called the devil, or Satan, who leads the whole world astray. He was hurled to the earth, and his angels with him.
>
> Then I heard a loud voice in heaven say:
>> "Now have come the salvation and the power
>>   and the kingdom of our God,
>>   and the authority of his Messiah.
>> For the accuser of our brothers and sisters,

who accuses them before our God day and night,
    has been hurled down.
They triumphed over him
    by the blood of the Lamb
    and by the word of their testimony;
they did not love their lives so much
    as to shrink from death.
Therefore rejoice, you heavens
    and you who dwell in them!
But woe to the earth and the sea,
    because the devil has gone down to you!
He is filled with fury,
    because he knows that his time is short" (Revelation 12:7–12).

Without unpacking a single line of this compacted war chronicle (which we will do later), it is already clear, is it not, that the battle thus waged is the one that rages fiercely in every human soul, the cosmic struggle for every man's allegiance, every woman's loyalty? And is it not more than evident that there are only two sides, the side of the blood of the Lamb versus the side of the fury of the dragon? Furthermore, does it not follow we are either on one side or the other, that there is no middle ground or third side?

I was talking with a young man recently who got sucked into the drug culture. It started off with a bit of weed . . . then prescription drugs not his own . . . then meth. And before he knew it, he was hooked. Perhaps you can sympathize with him. Perhaps we all can.

Speaking of this war we are all in, he described for me those moments of sobriety when the voice of God would speak to him and call him away from that bondage: "Come to me, all you who are weary and burdened, and I will give you rest" (Matthew 11:28).

But in that same instant, he explained, the dragon enemy of us all would suddenly "materialize" in his consciousness with the harsh voice of accusation:

- "You can't go back now—look at you—you're hopelessly addicted."
- "I mean, how many times have you asked God to deliver you, and He hasn't, now has He?"
- "You know why? Because you're a loser—that's why! God doesn't want a failure like you hanging around Him."

- "So why don't you just come with me and live the life you really enjoy—with no conscience to bother you anymore?"
- "He's not going to save you—it's too late!"
- "Come follow me instead."

As the young man described to me his struggle with this desperately real battle raging in his own mind, my eyes welled up as I realized how utterly brutalizing the bondage of "that ancient serpent called the devil, or Satan, who leads the whole world astray" can be. Accusing you, accusing me—there isn't one of us who hasn't heard these lines from "the accuser of our brothers and sisters," is there?

But the apocalyptic line that counts is terse but unequivocal: "They [the followers of Christ] triumphed over him [the malevolent dragon accuser] by the blood of the Lamb [Calvary] and by the word of their testimony; they did not love their lives so much as to shrink from death" (verse 11).

On the authority of that single revelation, that young man was *not* rejected by God. And he is *not* a loser. In fact, he is one of our young leaders in my congregation today. For he is living proof of this compelling promise in that short classic *Steps to Christ*:

> When Satan [the accuser] comes to tell you that you are a great sinner, look up to your Redeemer and talk of His merits. That which will help you is to look to His light. Acknowledge your sin, but tell the enemy that "Christ Jesus came into the world to save sinners" and that you may be saved by His matchless love. 1 Timothy 1:15. . . . We have been great sinners, but Christ died that we might be forgiven. . . . It is when we most fully comprehend the love of God that we best realize the sinfulness of sin. When we see the length of the chain that was let down for us, when we understand something of the infinite sacrifice that Christ has made in our behalf, the heart is melted with tenderness and contrition.[8]

So let doomscrolling the future begin. But let it begin with Revelation's twin baselines: this same Jesus is still center stage in the Apocalypse, and His crushing defeat of the enemy remains the triumphant promise of history past, present, and future. Whatever else we may discover, these two baselines must illumine the path to life and hope for America, for us all.

1. Sophie Bushwick, "How to Stop Doomscrolling News and Social Media," *Scientific American*, February 12, 2021, https://www.scientificamerican.com/article/how-to-stop-doomscrolling-news-and-social-media/.

2. See 2 John 1; 3 John 1.

3. Ranko Stefanovic, *Plain Revelation* (Berrien Springs, MI: Andrews University Press, 2013), 11; emphasis added.

4. Elizabeth Viera Talbot, *Jesus Wins!* (Nampa, ID: Pacific Press®, 2019).

5. Stefanovic, *Plain Revelation*, 11.

6. Ellen G. White, *Selected Messages*, book 1 (Washington, DC: Review and Herald®, 1958), 403.

7. Sigve Tonstad, *Revelation* (Grand Rapids, MI: Baker Academic, 2019), 21.

8. Ellen G. White, *Steps to Christ* (Washington, DC: Review and Herald®, 1956), 35, 36.

You do not have to be an economist

or a sociologist to understand that even

the perception of significant financial

and economic inequities in society (no

matter how they are calculated) has the

potential to ignite major social unrest.

"WHAT'S PAST IS PROLOGUE"

During the pandemic lockdown in 2020, I pulled out Charles Dickens's classic, *A Tale of Two Cities*, and read again this dramatic narrative set in London and Paris during the bloody French Revolution. I suppose the whole world knows its opening line, and you, too, could repeat it: "It was the best of times, it was the worst of times."[1]

Someone (probably an English major) printed a T-shirt with these words: "I wish you would make up your mind, Mr. Dickens. Was it the best of times or the worst of times? It could scarcely have been both." But as far as the French Revolution was concerned, it was both.

And as far as America today is concerned, it is the best of times and the worst of times. So we would do well to consider the story of 1790s France, out of concern for our 2020s America. Are the seeds of the French Revolution and its dreaded Reign of Terror embedded in our own story now? Is France's past our prologue? Or can we be spared its ending?

Society in France leading up to the bloody French Revolution consisted of three Estates, as they called them: The First Estate was the clergy; the Second Estate, the nobility; and the Third Estate consisted of the bourgeoisie, or middle class, and the lower classes down to the peasants. "The feudal stratification of society into three classes . . . had become unjust and illogical by the eighteenth century [the late 1700s]. In France, a country with perhaps twenty-five million people, the clergy and nobility constituted less than two per cent of the population, yet they enjoyed the income from the richest lands of the kingdom, were exempted from the most onerous taxes and occupied by right of rank the highest and best paid offices in the government, the army, and the church."[2]

You do not have to be an economist or a sociologist to understand that even the perception of significant financial and economic inequities in society (no matter how they are calculated) has the potential to ignite major social unrest.

"The heavy and unequal taxes were a special source of bitterness [in France]. All the ranks of the underprivileged, the upper middle class, the lower middle class, the artisans, the servants, the peasants, down to the thieves and vagabonds of the highway, hated the fiscal system. This was not surprising since the burden of taxation rested most heavily upon those least able to support it and crushed the peasant most cruelly of all."[3]

So it was with France on the eve of the French Revolution. And how is it with America today? *Rolling Stone* magazine carried this biting economic critique of American society:

> [In the 1950s] marginal tax rates for the wealthy were 90 percent. The salaries of CEOs were, on average, just 20 times that of their mid-management employees. Today, the base pay of those at the top is commonly 400 times that of their salaried staff, with many earning orders of magnitude more in stock options and perks. The elite one percent of Americans control $30 trillion of assets, while the bottom half have more debt than assets. The three richest Americans have more money than the poorest 160 million of their countrymen. Fully a fifth of American households have zero or negative net worth, a figure that rises to 37 percent for black families. The median wealth of black households is a tenth that of whites. The vast majority of Americans—white, black, and brown—are two paychecks removed from bankruptcy. Though living in a nation that celebrates itself as the wealthiest in history, most Americans live on a high wire, with no safety net to brace a fall.[4]

Two thousand years ago, the stepbrother of Jesus issued this ominous warning about economic disparity:

> Your wealth has rotted, and moths have eaten your clothes. Your gold and silver are corroded. Their corrosion will testify against you and eat your flesh like fire. You have hoarded wealth *in the last days*. Look! The wages you failed to pay the workers who mowed your fields are crying out against you. The cries of the harvesters have reached the ears of the Lord Almighty. You have lived on earth in luxury and self-indulgence. You have fattened yourselves in the day of slaughter. You have condemned and

murdered the innocent one, who was not opposing you (James 5:2–6; emphasis added).

France on the eve of the bloody French Revolution, America on the eve of who knows what anymore—was James writing of us, too? The similarities may be more than coincidental. But could they be predictive?

The writer Ellen White connects the warning of James to this moment in Earth's history:

> The Scriptures describe the condition of the world *just before Christ's second coming*. Of the men who by robbery and extortion are amassing great riches, it is written: "Ye have heaped treasure together for the last days. Behold, the hire of the laborers who have reaped down your fields, which is of you kept back by fraud, crieth: and the cries of them which have reaped are entered into the ears of the Lord of Sabaoth. Ye have lived in pleasure on the earth, and been wanton; ye have nourished your hearts, as in a day of slaughter. Ye have condemned and killed the just; and he doth not resist you."
>
> But who reads the warnings given by the fast-fulfilling signs of the times?[5]

Welcome to the apocalyptic world of scary, weird beasts. Nightmares and the book of Daniel are full of them, and Revelation is no different.

Then she issues her own withering critique of this nation's economic disparity: "By every species of oppression and extortion, men are piling up colossal fortunes, while the cries of starving humanity are coming up before God. There are multitudes struggling with poverty, compelled to labor hard for small wages, unable to secure the barest necessities of life. Toil and deprivation, with no hope of better things, make their burden heavy. When pain and sickness are added, the burden is almost unbearable."[6]

"This is a picture of what exists today."[7] In America.

And what was it that took France down? It was an economic system with its obscene divide between the haves and the have-nots. The French

Revolution exploded across the land when the impoverished people on the bottom rung of society banded together to throw off the hated yoke of economic oppression. It was a ragtag coalition of anarchists and revolutionaries that ignited the uprising, eventually bringing down the throne, the church, and the nobility. Their dreaded instrument of choice was what the insurrectionists called Madame la Guillotine. The Reign of Terror. *A Tale of Two Cities* is the story of innocent lives trapped in that web.

> America! America!
> God shed His grace on thee,
> And crown thy good with brotherhood
> From sea to shining sea.[8]

Will what brought France down bring America down? Probably not. It will be worse. And yet, how pristine America's storied beginning: "Then I saw a second beast, coming out of the earth. It had two horns like a lamb, but it spoke like a dragon" (Revelation 13:11).

Welcome to the apocalyptic world of scary, weird beasts. Nightmares and the book of Daniel are full of them, and Revelation is no different. And when beasts appear in apocalyptic prophecy, they symbolize great nations, empires, or kingdoms—world-changing powers.

What in the world is this earth-beast power or nation? Consider these clues:

Clue no. 1—It *sprang up.*

The Greek word here is *anabaino*, which is the same word Jesus uses in His parable of the sower to describe the thorny weeds that "sprang up" overnight (Matthew 13:7, NKJV). So whatever this power is, it comes suddenly onto the stage of history.

Clue no. 2—It sprang up from "the earth."

There are two beasts described in this apocalyptic vision. Revelation 13 opens with a sea beast crawling out of the briny waters of the ocean, dripping and ferocious: "Then the angel said to me, 'The waters you saw, where the prostitute sits, are peoples, multitudes, nations and languages' " (Revelation 17:15). We will get to the prostitute later, but notice the angel interpreter identifies waters as a symbol of people—Earth's multitudes and masses.

In contrast to the peopled and trafficked thoroughfares of the sea beast, the earth beast springs up like a weed out of the barren earth. No masses or multitudes there, just a desolate wilderness.

So far, two clues inform readers of the Apocalypse that here is a nation or power that sprang up suddenly in a desolate land far away from the thoroughfares of history.

Clue no. 3—"*Then* I saw a second beast, coming out of the earth."

"Then" means there is some sort of sequence transpiring in this unfolding prophetic scenario. First, there is a sea beast—"then" there springs up an earth beast. So the question is, What has transpired in this prophecy just before the "then"?

> Whoever has ears, let them hear.

> "If anyone is to go into captivity,
>   into captivity they will go.
> If anyone is to be killed with the sword,
>   with the sword they will be killed."

> This calls for patient endurance and faithfulness on the part of God's people (Revelation 13:9, 10).

Clearly, some power has been causing others to go into captivity—but now that power is itself taken into captivity. This same power that has been slaughtering others with the sword now is itself mortally wounded by the sword.

Bible scholars believe this sea beast symbolizes the ruling power during the Middle Ages: A power that would rule over European history for more than a millennium; a power that decimated the faithful of God, who at the supreme price of their own lives stood up to this institution.[9]

But suddenly, that ruthless geo-religio-political kingdom would be mortally wounded, as history bears out. For as it turns out, the French Revolution's Napoleon Bonaparte would be instrumental in bringing this power to its knees at the end of the 1700s, when he ordered the pope taken captive. Mortal wound indeed. Jacques Doukhan notes the irony:

> The French Revolution would confront the church with
> an atheistic society having but one god: reason. But most

important, in 1798 the French army under the commanding officer General Berthier would invade Rome, capture the pope, and deport him. General Bonaparte intended to eradicate papal and church authority. Ironically, it was France, the "eldest daughter of the Church," who had originally established the papacy as a political power. Now the nation would strip the pope of his prerogatives.[10]

And yet, at that same time, this earth beast would spring into existence in a barren land far from Europe's traveled crossroads. "*Then* I saw a second beast, coming out of the earth." So what power is this that sprang up suddenly in a desolate land far away from the crowded thoroughfares of Europe and did so at the end of the 1700s? Consider another clue.

Clue no. 4—"It had two horns like a lamb."

There is no question the shining Hero of the Apocalypse is "the Lamb who was slain from the creation of the world" (Revelation 13:8)—code language, as every believer in Jesus Christ knows, for Calvary's mighty Savior of this lost and fallen planet. He is the enthroned King of heaven, the One myriads of angels still sing over: "Worthy is the Lamb, who was slain, to receive power and wealth and wisdom and strength and honor and glory and praise" (Revelation 5:12). Only one Being in the universe deserves this seven-fold doxology!

It is this Hero Lamb the modifier "like a lamb" in Revelation 13:11 intimates. Whatever this earth-beast apocalyptic power is that springs up near the close of the 1700s, its lamblike features indicate a youthful and gentle-looking power that initially reflected the values of Christ, of Judeo-Christianity. At least, that is how it appeared at the beginning of its history.

Ranko Stefanovic concludes: "What power in the world does this lamb-like [earth] beast represent? There is only one world power that appeared in history in the post-medieval period that fits the description of the lamblike beast of Revelation 13: the Protestant United States. Revelation 13 shows that the United States of America, which in the post-medieval period provided protection and a safe haven for the church, will play the key role in last-day events."[11]

But before we examine its ominous prophesied future, we do well to pause and reflect on the profound "safe haven" this country has become for so many.

The apocalyptic classic *The Great Controversy* reminds us of those halcyon days at this country's beginning, now so far away and sadly bygone:

> As the tidings spread through the countries of Europe, of a land where every man might enjoy the fruit of his own labor and obey the convictions of his own conscience, thousands flocked to the shores of the New World. . . .
>
> The Bible was held as the foundation of faith, the source of wisdom, and the charter of liberty. Its principles were diligently taught in the home, in the school, and in the church, and its fruits were manifest in thrift, intelligence, purity, and temperance. . . . It was demonstrated that the principles of the Bible are the surest safeguards of national greatness. The feeble and isolated colonies grew to a confederation of powerful states, and the world marked with wonder the peace and prosperity of "a church without a pope, and a state without a king."[12]

Sadly those days are truly bygone. Consider the final clue.

Clue no. 5—"But it spoke like a dragon."

Jacques Doukhan warns:

> With its two little horns, the [earth] beast resembles a lamb (Rev. 13:11)—it can be trusted. . . . Yet we must not let it fool us. The lamb speaks like a dragon (Rev. 13:11). Such contradictory traits should shock us. Shattering its innocent and comforting image, the lamb suddenly roars like a dragon. The pieces of the puzzle come together to form an unexpected portrait. An economic and political superpower originating in the late eighteenth century, a haven for the religiously oppressed, the United States of America roars on the international scene like a dragon, yet displays the face of a lamb.[13]

A bipolar power this nation will become—part lamb, part dragon. And yet we can still sing: "God bless America, land that I love / Stand beside her and guide her / Through the night with the light from above."[14]

Because God *has* blessed this nation. In fact, the author of *The Great Controversy* described America's receipt of divine blessings this way: "The

Lord has done more for the United States than for any other country upon which the sun shines."[15] In any language, that is a largesse of blessings!

But those blessings have come at a price, a high price. Jesus Himself defined the divine standard of judgment in unmistakable terms: "From everyone who has been given much, much will be demanded; and from the one who has been entrusted with much, much more will be asked" (Luke 12:48). Which, being interpreted, means that on the great Judgment Day, this land of great gifts will have to answer for what she did with these bestowals of divine approbation. When America stands before Almighty God one day—with the wealth of the ages overflowing from her hands—He will quietly ask, "What did you do with all the blessings I showered upon you?" And what shall we say?

How did *Rolling Stone* magazine describe our bounties or the lack thereof?

- "The elite one percent of Americans control $30 trillion of assets, while the bottom half have more debt than assets."
- "The three richest Americans have more money than the poorest 160 million of their countrymen."
- "Fully a fifth of American households have zero or negative net worth, a figure that rises to 37 percent for black families."
- "The median wealth of black households is a tenth that of whites."
- "The vast majority of Americans—white, black, and brown—are two paychecks removed from bankruptcy. Though living in a nation that celebrates itself as the wealthiest in history, most Americans live on a high wire, with no safety net to brace a fall."[16]

In all candor, how can God go on blessing America with numbers like these? All the gifts He has poured out upon this nation, and they end up in a relatively few hands? It is a recipe for anger and anarchy, for rebellion and revolt.

It is France all over again. George McCready Price wisely cautions us:

We have been told that from our day onward the entire world is going to pass seriatim [step-by-step] through the successive stages of folly and horror that Paris went through on a small scale in a few short years. In other words, *France gave us a brief preview of what the entire world is now going through or will*

go through until the dragon's voice is heard in all its horror. . . .
"The same teachings that led to the French Revolution . . . are
tending to involve the whole world in a struggle similar to that
which convulsed France."—*Education*, p. 228.[17]

The atheism that sprang from the terror of the French Revolution
(think Voltaire and the Goddess of Reason) has long since claimed this
civilization's intellectual soul. And tragically enough, it is the baleful
harvest America now reaps in its third century of rule. What George
McCready Price calls the "anti-Genesis apostasy" has turned our schools
into godless institutions from kindergarten to graduate school.[18] No more
God, no more Creator, no more tolerance of Scripture. That was precisely
the fruit of the French Revolution.

And what about us? In France, marriage was reduced to a civil covenant
between anybody. In America, it is now the same—between anybody. In
France, the guillotine ran red with the slaughter of innocent lives. In America, the
slaughter of the innocents numbers in the millions of babies whose lives have been
terminated before birth—or even worse, after birth.

Something has happened to the soul of America. And it is *not* good. And all the
talk we hear about the iron fist of law and order will not heal the moral sickness that
chokes America's soul. You can't enforce salvation. We who have been given much now shut the rest
of the world out and hoard our riches for our own pleasure and profit.
All the while, inside our closed-off borders, human beings are suffering
of want and hunger. Just like France before the revolution, the wealthy
grow wealthier. Until the downtrodden rise up and storm the Bastille.

It turns out William Shakespeare was prescient when, in *The Tempest*,
he penned the line: "What's past is prologue."[19] As it turns out, the past
of long-ago France was but a prologue to America's fractured story today.
Is there any hope?

In truth, there is only one moral solution for the United States. And that is for this nation to turn back to the Creator God who superintended its founding 250 years ago. The solution does not lie in the creation of a national church or an alliance of churches, synagogues, and mosques. America's only hope lies in the Creator Himself, who surely is able to save this land from national ruin and self-destruction.

In the pages ahead, we will examine what this moral solution might look like. But could it be that the words of the beloved patriotic hymn may yet point us to the way?

America! America!
God shed His grace on thee
And crown thy good with brotherhood
From sea to shining sea.[20]

Therein lies our only hope.

---

1. Charles Dickens, *A Tale of Two Cities* (New York: Dell Publishing, 1963), 11.

2. Wallace K. Ferguson and Geoffrey Bruun, *A Survey of European History* (Boston: Houghton Mifflin, 1969), 561–563.

3. Wallace K. Ferguson and Geoffrey Bruun, *Survey of European Civilization,* ed. Carl Lotus Becker (New York: Houghton Mifflin, 1936), 125.

4. Wade Davis, "The Unraveling of America," *Rolling Stone*, August 6, 2020, https://www.rollingstone.com/politics/political-commentary/covid-19-end-of-american-era-wade-davis-1038206/. Davis is an anthropologist and holds the BC Leadership Chair in Cultures and Ecosystems at Risk at the University of British Columbia.

5. Ellen G. White, *Testimonies for the Church*, vol. 9 (Mountain View, CA: Pacific Press®, 1948), 13, 14; emphasis added.

6. White, 9:90, 91.

7. White.

8. Katharine Lee Bates, "America the Beautiful" (1893).

9. We will examine more closely the sea beast and the ancient and contemporary power it represents in subsequent chapters.

10. Jacques Doukhan, *Secrets of Daniel: Wisdom and Dreams of a Jewish Prince* (Hagerstown, MD: Review and Herald, 2000), 109, 110.

11. Ranko Stefanovic, *Plain Revelation* (Berrien Springs, MI: Andrews University Press, 2013), 160.

12. Ellen G. White, *The Great Controversy* (Mountain View, CA: Pacific Press®, 1950), 296.

13. Jacques Doukhan, *Secrets of Revelation: The Apocalypse Through Hebrew Eyes* (Hagerstown, MD: Review and Herald®, 2002), 118, 119.

14. Irving Berlin, "God Bless America" (Winthrop Rutherford Jr., Anne Phipps Sidamon-Eristoff, and Theodore R. Jackson as trustees of the God Bless America Fund, 1965, 1966).

15. Ellen G. White, *Maranatha* (Washington, DC: Review and Herald®, 1976), 193.

16. Davis, "Unraveling of America."

17. George McCready Price, *Time of the End* (Nashville, TN: Southern Publishing Association, 1967), 54, 55; emphasis in the original.

18. Price wrote: "Many do not realize that the scientific philosophy of evolution is merely a more polite and disguised form of the same power [organized atheism], which we have named the modern anti-Genesis apostacy." *Time of the End*, 55.

19. Wikipedia, s.v. "What's Past Is Prologue," last modified February 17, 2020, https://en.wikipedia.org/wiki/What%27s_past_is_prologue.

20. Katharine Lee Bates, "America the Beautiful" (1893).

Long before there was war in our marriages

and families, before there was war in our

cities and streets, before there

was war in our nation and war on our

planet, before our own private histories of

heartache, the truth was and still is—war

first broke out in heaven and broke the

heart of the Father of us all.

HOW TO TRAIN YOUR DRAGON

A young schoolboy was racing for the bus one morning. Panting and gasping for air, he arrived at the bus stop just in time to see the taillights disappear around the corner. A bystander who saw it all remarked, "Too bad, son—you just didn't run fast enough."

"Oh no, sir, I ran fast enough," the honest boy answered, still gulping for air. "I just didn't start soon enough."

In all candor, therein lies the mounting concern for this nation, this civilization. Perhaps we can run fast enough. But I fear we won't start soon enough.

The burgeoning litany of humanity's woes—from the COVID-19 pandemic that is still rewriting our playbooks for almost every major facet of human life and medical survival on this planet; to the radioactive debates over mounting greenhouse gases and climate change and global warming; to the dwindling resources of drinkable water and sustainable food crops in both the United States and the Two-Thirds World; to the yawning chasm between the wealthy and the impoverished and the festering divide between East and West, blacks and whites, Muslims and Christians, Jews and Palestinians; to collapsing moral standards battered into retreat by unbridled sexual license. Headlines like these and more now expose a civilization intractably imprisoned in a rapidly disintegrating world.

Here are some numbers precipitously stacking against us.

"Within the lifetime of anyone born at the start of the Baby Boom, the human population has tripled. Has this resulted in a human endeavor three times better—or one-third as capable of surviving? In the 1960s, humans took about three-quarters of what the planet could regenerate annually. By 2016 this rose to 170 percent, meaning that the planet cannot keep up with human demand, and we are running the world down."[1] Even if these scientists are only half right, we would still be in a heap of trouble. But keep reading.

" 'In other words,' say 17 of the world's leading ecologists in a stark new perspective on our place in life and time, 'humanity is running an ecological Ponzi scheme in which society robs nature and future generations to pay for boosting incomes in the short term.' Their starkly titled article, 'Underestimating the Challenges of Avoiding a Ghastly Future,' reads less as an argument than as a rain of asteroids encountered in the course of flying blind on a lethal trajectory."[2] Colorful simile, strong warning.

The truth is, we are in a systemic planetary war—and the battle is intensifying! Commenting on global conditions just before His return, Jesus described the intensification this way:

> For then there will be great distress, unequaled from the beginning of the world until now—and never to be equaled again.
> If those days had not been cut short, no one would survive, but for the sake of the elect those days will be shortened (Matthew 24:21, 22).

Not exactly a "sweet by-and-by" ending to this civilization, is it?

The Apocalypse unabashedly identifies the perpetrator of this dark, worldwide intensification. Call it entropy or system-wide collapse; we know the "first causer." All you have to do is read beyond the words "And there was war in heaven" (Revelation 12:7, KJV). Though you must admit that that terse war-in-heaven announcement is in and of itself beyond shocking in its implications! Do you mean to say *that* heaven—the seat of the God-is-love Deity who rules the universe? There was war in *that* heaven? Yes, the Apocalypse solemnly nods.

But it is in this war-in-heaven truth that we humans may yet find a modicum of comfort. For long before there was war in our marriages and families, before there was war in our cities and streets, before there was war in our nation and war on our planet, before our own private histories of heartache, the truth was and still is—war first broke out in heaven and broke the heart of the Father of us all. *Even in God's perfect family, war broke out.* We are not alone. Someone else understands our embattled hurt.

Read it again for yourself:

> Then war broke out in heaven. Michael and his angels fought against the dragon, and the dragon and his angels fought back. But he was not strong enough, and they lost their place

in heaven. The great dragon was hurled down—that ancient serpent called the devil, or Satan, who leads the whole world astray. He was hurled to the earth, and his angels with him (Revelation 12:7–9).

And who is this heavenly being named Michael—whose ancient name means "Who is like God" (which can be a question or a statement)? Clearly, He is an apocalyptic Warrior. For He appears only in the three apocalyptic books of the Bible (Daniel 10:13, 21; 12:1; Jude 9; Revelation 12:7), and He appears only in warfare passages. There is a long line of Reformation proponents, from Melanchthon and onward, who have identified Michael as the apocalyptic depiction of the pre-incarnate Christ.

Are you suggesting Christ is or was an angel? Not at all. But it is not that much of a stretch to conclude that Christ, the mighty Second Person of the triune God—the eternal Creator of the universe and all that is in it (John 1:1–3; Colossians 1:16, 17; Hebrews 1:2), who "became flesh and made his dwelling among us" (John 1:14)—could have taken the form of an angel on occasion, even as He has now embraced the form of a human. After all, angels and humans: Did He not create them both? And was not the Angel of the Lord who appeared throughout the Old Testament often the manifestation of God Himself (e.g., Genesis 16:7, 13; Exodus 3:2–6)? So then it is no great leap of logic to conclude Michael was the Angel of the Lord, the Commander of heaven's angels, is it?

Sigve Tonstad shapes a moving point about Jesus as Michael: "This means that a divine figure can be represented in angelic terms without being an angel . . . . Perhaps Jesus does not mind being represented as an angel or even thought of as one? Why would it offend him to be represented as an angel when he is not bothered by being a human? To appear lower in rank than he is and not consider it shameful is consonant with the disposition of Jesus (Heb. 2:11–12; Phil. 2:5–12), and the commitment is irreversible."[3] How like Him to so closely identify with those He leads.

So, Michael we know. And the dragon, who is he?

As it turns out, our culture has gone gaga over dragons—thanks to DreamWorks and Disney, we can picture them in all their graphic gore or lore. In 2010, DreamWorks came out with an animated movie entitled *How to Train Your Dragon*—the sweet story of a friendly dragon befriended by a boy who just didn't fit in and a girl who came to like the boy who liked the dragon. But if you prefer more roar than romance, there is always Smaug, the fire-breathing dragon of J. R. R. Tolkien's colorful imagination. And besides, who believes in dragons anyway? That question, of course, could turn out to be a brilliant bit of demonic strategy, crafted to lead "wise" humans to laugh away the devil and the demonic as figments of ancient folklore and imagination.

The Apocalypse is clear. The dragon is Revelation's dramatic, crimson, seven-headed and ten-crowned symbol of *"that ancient serpent called the devil, or Satan, who leads the whole world astray"* (Revelation 12:9; emphasis added).

C. S. Lewis was right:

> As it turns out, our culture has gone gaga over dragons—thanks to DreamWorks and Disney, we can picture them in all their graphic gore or lore.

One of the things that surprised me when I first read the New Testament seriously was that it talked so much about a Dark Power in the universe—a mighty evil spirit who was held to be the Power behind death and disease, and sin. . . . Christianity thinks this Dark Power was created by God, and was good when he was created, and went wrong. Christianity agrees with Dualism that this universe is at war. But it does not think this is a war between independent powers. It thinks it is a civil war, a rebellion, and that we are living in a part of the universe occupied by the rebel. Enemy-occupied territory—that is what this world is.[4]

But there is more to this apocalyptic dragon. Consider these breathtaking portrayals of who he was before he became so dragon-like, as recorded in Ezekiel 28:

- "You were the seal of perfection, full of wisdom and perfect in beauty" (verse 12).
- "You were in Eden, the garden of God . . . on the day you were created" (verse 13).
- "You were anointed as a guardian cherub, for so I ordained you. You were on the holy mount of God; you walked among the fiery stones" (verse 14).
- "You were blameless in your ways from the day you were created

till wickedness was found in you" (verse 15).
- "So I drove you in disgrace from the mount of God, and I expelled you, guardian cherub, from among the fiery stones" (verse 16).
- "Your heart became proud on account of your beauty, and you corrupted your wisdom because of your splendor. So I threw you to the earth" (verse 17).

Here is an angelic being, perfect in all his ways, until the mystery of pride sprang up within his secret soul and destroyed the high destiny of this God-created cherub—the highest-ranking angel, who guarded the very throne of the Divine and was thus dramatically expelled: "I threw you to the earth." Every detail here echoes in the apocalyptic portrayal of war in heaven.

But there is more. In full accord with Ezekiel's spiritual postmortem of the fallen angel, notice now Isaiah's probing analysis of this being's self-destructive pride (count the five *I*'s):

How you have fallen from heaven,
   morning star ["Lucifer" in the KJV], son of the dawn!
You have been cast down to the earth,
   you who once laid low the nations!
You said in your heart,
   "I will ascend to the heavens;
I will raise my throne
   above the stars of God;
I will sit enthroned on the mount of assembly,
   on the utmost heights of Mount Zaphon.
I will ascend above the tops of the clouds;
   I will make myself like the Most High" (Isaiah 14:12–14).

Only the insanity of pride could lead a creature to set out to become Creator! Insane, for how could a child become his Father? Such was (and still is) the insanity of ego. It corrupted the shining prime minister of heaven who stood beside the Eternal, debasing that angel into the veritable rebel dragon, at war now with all of heaven. And Earth.

What triggered such a tragic revolt within heaven's family? Could it be that Michael, the King of heaven, was Himself in the form of an angel, and that might have suggested to Lucifer his grasp for Michael's position on the throne was a shorter reach than first thought? *Why can't*

I be like the Most High? After all, am I not an angel just like He? Such a thought, though irrational, could have triggered Lucifer's tragic fall.

The Great Controversy draws aside the veil to Lucifer's tempted heart:

> Sin originated with him who, next to Christ, had been most honored of God and who stood highest in power and glory among the inhabitants of heaven. . . .
>
> . . . This prince of angels aspired to power which it was the prerogative of Christ [Michael] alone to wield. . . .
>
> . . . In all the counsels of God, Christ was a participant, while Lucifer was not permitted thus to enter into the divine purposes.[5]

Thus, seeds of envy, pride, and self-worship were mysteriously planted in Lucifer's heart—by Lucifer's own hand.

And the rest is history, the sad and tragic history of a universe torn apart by an internecine war (or, in Greek, *polemos*) of competing ideologies and battling allegiances—a cosmic war of words and ideas—a polemical battle pitting self-worship against self-sacrifice, self-asserting ambition against self-emptying love. Love was bound to win, of course. But no one but Love could know how high and infinite the price would turn out to be.

"He [the dragon] was hurled to the earth, and his angels with him" (Revelation 12:9).

There is something else you need to know about this expelled-to-earth rebel angel. And that is he is no dragon. With the snap of his angelic finger, he can transform himself into a being of dazzling light (see 2 Corinthians 11:14). But it's all a sham and fake. In fact, contemplate for a moment what feels very much like an eyewitness account of what he looks like right now.

> I was shown Satan as he once was, a happy, exalted angel. Then I was shown him as he now is. He still bears a kingly form. His features are still noble, for he is an angel fallen. But the expression of his countenance is full of anxiety, care, unhappiness, malice, hate, mischief, deceit, and every evil. That brow which was once so noble, I particularly noticed. His forehead commenced from his eyes to recede. I saw that he had so long bent himself to evil that every good quality was debased, and every evil trait was developed. His eyes were cunning, sly, and

showed great penetration. His frame was large, but the flesh hung loosely about his hands and face. As I beheld him, his chin was resting upon his left hand. He appeared to be in deep thought. A smile was upon his countenance, which made me tremble, it was so full of evil and satanic slyness. This smile is the one he wears just before he makes sure of his victim, and as he fastens the victim in his snare, this smile grows horrible.[6]

Let it be repeated: There is something you need to know about the dragon. First, he is no dragon at all. And second, he is driven to frenzy when an earth child calls on the blood of the Lamb for deliverance. "They [the followers of Christ] triumphed over him [the dragon] by the blood of the Lamb and by the word of their testimony" (Revelation 12:11).

Because the Lamb of God is none other than the incarnated Creator, who infiltrated this world. As C. S. Lewis described him, "The rightful king [who] landed, you might say landed in disguise, and is calling us all to take part in a great campaign of sabotage."[7] Immanuel, "God with us," was mysteriously birthed onto this rebel planet to win the heart of humanity back to the Father of us all. "The Word became flesh and made his dwelling among us" (John 1:14). And so, He ate with us and slept with us, wept with us and laughed with us, and all the while told us stories of God, who is not somebody to be afraid of but someone to be a friend of.

> Satan is driven to frenzy when an earth child calls upon the blood of the Lamb for deliverance.

But Lucifer would have none of it. He may have lost his place in heaven, but he tenaciously lays claim to this planet and will fight to the death to hold it. Remember the temptations of Christ? In the third temptation, Satan (pretending to be a dazzling angel of light) revealed to the emaciated Jesus "all the kingdoms of the world and their splendor. 'All this I will give you,' he said, 'if you will bow down and worship me' " (Matthew 4:8, 9).

Imagine that! The fake prince of the world attempts to induce the incarnated King of kings to cravenly bow down before him and admit that Lucifer (heaven's documented loser) is the rightful king of Earth. What craziness now infects the fallen rebel!

But not even the barbaric torture of the Roman legionnaires could scourge or crucify the Son of God into abandoning His mission and forsake this hell-bent planet. When on the cross Jesus rent the awful funereal darkness of Golgotha with that piercing, naked scream, "My God, my God, why have you forsaken me?" (Matthew 27:46), we knew at last Love's infinite price in this bloody war. He was willing to die forever in order to give lost human beings the chance to live forever. In the words of Charles Wesley,

> Amazing love!
> How can it be
> That Thou, my God, shouldst die for me?[8]

And when His battered head raised back up in that pent-up death cry—"It is finished" (John 19:30)—then began to clang the triumphant death knell of the dragon's kingdom, a wild pealing that still resounds across the canyons and chasms of God's universe today.

Then I heard a loud voice in Heaven say:

> "Now have come the salvation and the power
>   and the kingdom of our God,
>   and the authority of his Messiah.
> For the accuser of our brothers and sisters,
>   who accuses them before our God day and night,
>   has been hurled down" (Revelation 12:10).

"In the Saviour's expiring cry, 'It is finished,' the death knell of Satan was rung. The great controversy which had been so long in progress was then decided, and the final eradication of evil was made certain."[9]

I was preaching in Sacramento, California. The Friday evening meeting was soon to begin when I spotted a young man walking down the aisle of the church, headed toward the front row where I was seated. He was wearing a black T-shirt—and across his shirt in huge bright red letters was the name SATAN. My eyes widened. What kind of a meeting was this going to be? But he kept coming my way, and finally, I saw a smile on his face as he extended a handshake. Then it was that I could read the T-shirt's small print below the red SATAN. In tiny white letters were these two words—is defeated.

Should you ever decide to put the three words *Satan is defeated* on a T-shirt, may I offer this personal suggestion: put the name Satan in really tiny letters at the top and under it, in letters so huge that all can read them from afar those two exultant words, Is DEFEATED! *That* was the triumphant message of Calvary. And *that* is precisely how the friends of Jesus still triumph over the defeated dragon and his legions.

On the cross, Jesus crushed the dark grip of the devil on you and me and the entire human race—He broke the dragon's grip to set us free!

This means you can pray this prayer every single day of your life:

> When Pilate saw that he could not prevail at all, but rather that a tumult was rising, he took water and washed his hands before the multitude, saying, "I am innocent of the blood of this just Person. You see to it."

When on the cross Jesus rent the awful funereal darkness of Golgotha with that piercing, naked scream, "My God, my God, why have you forsaken me?" (Matthew 27:46), we knew at last Love's infinite price in this bloody war. He was willing to die forever in order to give lost human beings the chance to live forever.

And all the people answered and said, "His blood be on us and on our children" (Matthew 27:24, 25, NKJV).

What if we turned what was meant to be a thoughtless but still tragic acceptance of responsibility into a thoughtful, even fervent prayer of blessing? What if when we called upon God, we appealed to Him in the name of our Lord Jesus? "His blood be on us and on our children." It is a short and simple prayer, but what a powerful petition for the power of our triumphant Savior to deliver us from evil and the evil one:

- Pray, "His blood be on me" if there is just one of you.
- Pray, "His blood be on us" if there are two of you.
- Pray, "His blood be on us and our children" if there are more of you.

What if every morning, as you begin your day, you prayed this prayer that appeals for the blood of the Lamb to be on you no matter what the dragon has in store for you? Want to know how effective such a prayer is?

> The truth is, the Hero of Heaven who went to the cross for you and me loves us too deeply to leave us unwarned.

"Dear brother, dear sister, when Satan would fill your mind with despondency, gloom, and doubt, resist his suggestions. *Tell him of the blood of Jesus*, that cleanses from all sin. You cannot save yourself from the tempter's power, but he trembles and flees when the merits of that precious blood are urged."[10]

Maybe it's time we tore a page out of the children of Israel's playbook. Remember how on the eve of the Exodus, they took the blood of a lamb and splashed it on the lintels and doorposts of their houses? Why? So the destroying angel would "pass over" them.

So what if we did the same? What if, in our mind's eye, we go to our laptop and smartphone and splash the blood of the Lamb on their screens to ensure that all we view or listen to through their high-tech wizardry would be protected from the dragon's insidious ways of penetrating our minds, our souls? Did you know that the blood of the Lamb can keep pornography off that screen?

What if we went to our refrigerator to splash the blood of the Lamb on its shelves, so all we eat or drink from there would be protected from the dragon's cunning strategies to destroy our bodies, minds, and hearts?

What if we go to our social media platforms, our video games, our ebooks, our DVD collections, our music files . . . you get the picture. Can you think of a better way to overcome the dragon by the blood of the Lamb than by graphic actionable symbolism like this?

For those who may be protesting—"Aw, c'mon, there's gotta be something left for me to enjoy"—I hope this doesn't come as an unwelcome shock to you, but *the party is over!* It is over for America. Just look at the mess we're in. It is over for the planet with its inexorable crises. And it needs to be over for you and me.

Look, I'm not saying we can't live life to the absolute full with joy and gladness and fresh hope for every new day with Jesus. But if our aim is to keep trying to turn life into nonstop fun and games and raucous craziness, we are only being duped by the cunning dragon who desperately seeks to keep us distracted so that we don't really know what time it is, so that we don't have the time to get serious about getting ready.

"We are living in the most solemn period of this world's history. The destiny of Earth's teeming multitudes [you and me] is about to be decided. . . . We need to humble ourselves before the Lord, with fasting and prayer, and to meditate much upon His word."[11]

Oh, how boring! Well, what did you want to be told? "The planet is on the eve of destruction, so let's pretend it's still party time as usual"?

When I was running the other day, I saw a sign outside a little church here in town: "The party in hell has been canceled—due to fire." This nation and this planet are about to go up in smoke—and you'd rather party? Give God a break!

The truth is, the Hero of heaven who went to the cross for you and me loves us too deeply to leave us unwarned. If in the night your house were on fire and you didn't know it, wouldn't you want someone who spotted it to pound on your door until somebody inside woke up? A response of "Leave me alone" would be the kiss of death, would it not?

So why put off coming under the complete protection of the blood of the Lamb? Pray that prayer. Paint your doorposts. I know we can run fast enough. But I fear we won't start soon enough, which begins right now.

1. Carl Safina, "Avoiding a 'Ghastly Future': Hard Truths on the State of the Planet," *Yale Environment 360*, January 27, 2021, https://e360.yale.edu/features/avoiding-a-ghastly-future-hard-truths-on-the-state-of-the-planet.

2. Safina.

3. Sigve Tonstad, *Revelation* (Grand Rapids, MI: Baker Academic, 2019), 48.

4. C. S. Lewis, *Mere Christianity* (New York: Macmillan, 1960), 50, 51.

5. Ellen G. White, *The Great Controversy* (Mountain View, CA: Pacific Press®, 1950), 493–495.

6. Ellen G. White, *Early Writings* (Washington, DC: Review and Herald®, 1945), 152, 153.

7. Lewis, *Mere Christianity*, 51.

8. Charles Wesley, "And Can It Be?" (1738).

9. White, *Great Controversy*, 503.

10. Ellen G. White, *Testimonies for the Church*, vol. 5 (Mountain View, CA: Pacific Press®, 1948), 317; emphasis added.

11. White, *Great Controversy*, 601.

Stunning, really, this profound declaration

from the risen Christ that what is done to

His followers on Earth, to the church He

left behind when He returned to heaven,

is done to Him.

THE BRIDE AND THE STREETWALKER

I cannot imagine what it would be like to be stoned to death, though I do know something about head-to-concrete blackout. As a ten-year-old who had just learned how to water-ski slalom style (i.e., with one ski), I was having the ski of my life when I nearly lost my life. I held on to the ski boat's towrope too long when skiing back to the pier, lost control, and skied headfirst into one of the pier's concrete abutments. Blackout![1]

Not only can I not imagine being stoned to death but I also can't fathom standing beside the stoning, watching that slow-motion death as a legal witness. But Saul, the young rabbi from Jerusalem, did. He stood there superintending the execution of Stephen, the also young and brilliant apologist and follower of the also executed Jesus of Nazareth. Perhaps to stifle his own conscience, Saul immediately set out to wipe out the fledgling community of believers in Christ wherever he could ferret them out. It was a bloody persecution.

Now, with a contingent of temple guards, Saul is riding northward to Damascus to snuff out any heretics who may have fled to that ancient bastion. Within sight of the walled city, Saul experiences what can only be described as a blinding nuclear explosion, brighter than the sun above him, hurling him to the ground.

With dust in his mouth from his fall, his eyes burned out from the explosion of light, Saul struggles to rise from the ground. Then a Voice breaks the sonic barrier high above him: "Saul, Saul." The Voice repeats his name as if to make sure the now-blinded rabbi is concentrating. Saul hears every word. "Who are you, Lord?" Lord? He calls Him Lord? But then, who else but the Divine could have exploded into such consciousness? The Voice answers. And it is for the answer we recall this dramatic moment of sacred history. *I am Jesus, whom you are persecuting* (Acts 9:5; emphasis added).

Stunning, really, this profound declaration from the risen Christ that what is done to His followers on Earth, to the church He left behind when He returned to heaven, is done to Him. "I am Jesus, whom you are persecuting." That describes but one reality. So close is God to His church, His people, that what anyone (singular or plural) does to them, it is done to Him—to the Lord Jesus Himself. "I am Jesus, whom you are persecuting." That is, "What you do to My church, you do to Me."

And that is what rings with such compelling clarity from the pages of the Apocalypse.

"One thing will certainly be understood from the study of Revelation— that the connection between God and His people is close and decided."[2] Whatever the dragon does to you, he does to Jesus. When they persecute you for your faith, they persecute Jesus. When they mock you for your convictions, they mock Jesus. When they attack the church you belong to, they attack Jesus. So close is God to His church, His people, that what anyone does to them, they do to Him—to the Lord Jesus Himself!

And nowhere in the Apocalypse could that be clearer than the stunning prophecy embedded in Revelation 12.

> A great sign appeared in heaven: a woman clothed with the sun, with the moon under her feet and a crown of twelve stars on her head. She was pregnant and cried out in pain as she was about to give birth. Then another sign appeared in heaven: an enormous red dragon with seven heads and ten horns and seven crowns on its heads. Its tail swept a third of the stars out of the sky and flung them to the earth. The dragon stood in front of the woman who was about to give birth, so that it might devour her child the moment he was born. She gave birth to a son, a male child, who "will rule all the nations with an iron scepter." And her child was snatched up to God and to his throne (verses 1–5).

What you have just read is apocalyptic prophecy at its classic best. Strange and scary images, creatures from a twilight zone we never occupy, often blend with the common and mundane—is there anyone who can't picture a pregnant woman?—concocted into a storyline or plot often bizarre but nonetheless traceable.

So what do we have in scene 1? A beautiful woman (in my humble opinion, pregnant women are always beautiful by virtue of the human and divine mission they fulfill in bringing another life into existence), wrapped in sunlight while she stands on the moon, a garland (in Greek, the word *stephanos*—a leafy laurel crown awarded to the victor—from whence came the name Stephen, the martyr) of twelve stars upon her brow. Beautiful indeed. And a salivating crimson dragon with seven crowned and roaring heads covered with ten spiked horns (grist for nightmares). We come upon the woman and the dragon moments before she is to give birth. In fact, her labor pains have already begun. And as only apocalyptic prophecy can do, the red dragon, with its seven heads all staring at this labor-intensive moment, is licking its seven salivating lips in anticipation (now this gets a bit gross) of devouring the child the moment it is birthed.[3]

Sigve Tonstad describes this scene as "the Maternity Ward of the Ages."[4] And sure enough, the Baby is born, a Man-child destined to rule "all the nations with an iron scepter" (Revelation 12:5), a royal symbol of the promised Messiah.[5]

Even a cursory reading of this prophecy quickly signals the connection between the apocalyptic woman and her newborn son with Mary and the Christ child. But it is the shortest Christmas story on record, for the moment the Man-child is born, He "is snatched up to God and to his throne" (Revelation 12:5). Surely somebody should be cheering—"You lose, red dragon! Missed again . . . big-time!" But the story isn't finished.

Now the dragon we have already met, this crimson monster symbol of the fallen Satan. But who is this beautiful woman who is no longer pregnant? Tonstad suggests that "the woman is a composite figure, carrying within herself elements of Eve, the community of faith, Israel, and even the Virgin Mary. . . . John tells the story in a *telescoped* fashion, many layers of narrative and long eons of time compressed into one decisive moment."[6]

But now the plot thickens: "The woman fled into the wilderness to a place prepared for her by God, where she might be taken care of for 1,260 days" (Revelation 12:6).

Before we take another step, consider for a moment the Bible's symbolic or metaphoric depiction of a woman, a pure woman, a woman of shining light as Revelation portrays her. What does she represent?

> Clue no. 1—"As a young man marries a young woman, so will your Builder marry you; as a bridegroom rejoices over his bride, so will your God rejoice over you" (Isaiah 62:5). The prophet Isaiah depicts the faith community of the Old Testament as the bride of God.

> Clue no. 2—"I am jealous for you with a godly jealousy. I promised you to one husband, to Christ, so that I might

present you as a pure virgin to him" (2 Corinthians 11:2). The apostle Paul, like Isaiah, depicts the faith community of the New Testament as the bride of Christ.

Clue no. 3—"Husbands, love your wives, just as Christ loved the church and gave himself up for her" (Ephesians 5:25). Once again, with even more definitive language, Paul describes the church as the bride of Christ.

Who is the woman in Revelation 12? It is clear the Bible utilizes a pure woman as a symbol of God's people on Earth, with God or Christ as the bridegroom. The pure and chaste woman of Revelation 12 represents that bride, the genuine faith community on Earth throughout its long history—in the Old Testament, in the New Testament, throughout the millennia until Christ returns.

But be forewarned. There are two women in the Apocalypse. And we dare not confuse them. Examine for a moment the Bible's dramatic use of an impure woman as a metaphor or symbol.

Clue no. 1—"When the LORD began to speak through Hosea, the LORD said to him, 'Go, marry a promiscuous woman and have children with her, for like an adulterous wife this land is guilty of unfaithfulness to the LORD' " (Hosea 1:2). The prophet Hosea describes Israel, when she was a fallen faith community in the Old Testament, as a promiscuous woman (a prostitute or adulteress).

Clue no. 2—"My people consult a wooden idol, and a diviner's rod speaks to them. A spirit of prostitution leads them astray; they are unfaithful to their God" (Hosea 4:12). Ancient Israel turned away from the Creator God to worship the idol gods of its neighbors. God describes that apostasy as "a spirit of prostitution." In fact, in Ezekiel 23:1–5, God compares Israel and Judah as sister prostitutes, so tragic had become Israel's fall for their neighbors' gods.

Clue no. 3—"One of the seven angels who had the seven bowls came and said to me, 'Come, I will show you the punishment of the great prostitute, who sits by many waters. With her the

kings of the earth committed adultery, and the inhabitants of
the earth were intoxicated with the wine of her adulteries. . . .

. . . The woman was dressed in purple and scarlet, and was
glittering with gold, precious stones and pearls. She held a
golden cup in her hand, filled with abominable things and the
filth of her adulteries. The name written on her forehead was
a mystery:

BABYLON THE GREAT
THE MOTHER OF PROSTITUTES
AND OF THE ABOMINATIONS OF THE EARTH.

I saw that the woman was drunk with the blood of God's holy
people, the blood of those who bore testimony to Jesus. When
I saw her, I was greatly astonished (Revelation 17:1, 2, 4–6).

She might as well have put on stilettos for her streetwalking! There she
is in the New Testament, this disturbing symbol of a whore or prostitute
to depict an apostate, counterfeit, or fallen church.

Clearly, the Bible describes two kinds of women to depict two kinds
of faith communities: a pure, noble woman to represent the bride of
God, His true and redeemed church (as we see her in Revelation 12),
and an impure, adulterous woman to represent the paramour or lover of
the dragon, a counterfeit and fallen church (as we see her in Revelation
17). Beware! In reality, the drama of Revelation is the play and counterplay
between these two women throughout the history of Christianity, a bloody
conflict we will be tracking.

But for the moment, we must return to the pure woman, the bride or
faith community of Christ, the New Testament church. We left her with
the roaring dragon who, having lost his chance to destroy the Messiah,
in rage turns to destroy the woman instead.

"The woman fled into the wilderness to a place prepared for her by God,
where she might be taken care of for 1,260 days" (Revelation 12:6).

A time packet of 1,260 days—what's this all about? Welcome to the
world of apocalyptic prophecy, where not only beasts from the earth and
sea and even women are interpreted symbolically, but so often, time itself
is expressed symbolically. Actually, this time packet is one of the most
familiar in Bible prophecy. Here it is expressed as 1,260 days (Revelation
12:6). In the previous chapter, this same time packet is expressed as both
1,260 days and 42 months (Revelation 11:2, 3).[7] And later in Revelation

12, it is calculated as "time [a year], times [2 years] and half a time [half a year]," or 3½ years (Revelation 12:14).[8] Formed as an equation, this time packet is expressed these three ways: 1,260 days = 42 months = 3½ years.

Further heightening the intrigue of apocalyptic prophecy is this significant and interpretive key—one prophetic day represents one literal year. It is an even swap. In fact, Bible scholars speak of "a day for a year."

The English mathematician Isaac Newton, himself a student of Bible prophecy, utilized this "time key" to interpret prophecies in both Daniel and Revelation. But actually, it was God who formulated this time key, as He told the children of Israel: "For forty years—one year for each of the forty days you explored the land—you will suffer for your sins [by wandering the wilderness before entering the Promised Land]" (Numbers 14:34). There it is—"a day for a year." Then to the young prophet Ezekiel, God declares:

> I have assigned you the same number of days as the years of their sin. . . .
> . . . a day for each year" (Ezekiel 4:5, 6).

There it is again—"a day for a year."

So when the raging dragon turns on the woman, who flees into the wilderness to hide from her enemy for 1,260 days—John is telling us in apocalyptic code language that she would be in hiding for 1,260 years. Again, 1,260 days in prophecy is the equivalent of 1,260 years in history.

And scholars are quite agreed that this time packet of 1,260 years is none other than the Middle Ages of church history. A period so dark, so oppressive that it appeared God's genuine faith community, God's true church, His chosen people on Earth would be decimated and wiped from the face of the earth.

Why? Because the other woman—the prostitute woman, the whore of the Apocalypse—was desperately seeking to eradicate every trace of opposition to her deceptive and bloody rule. But one woman stood in her way of total domination. Thus, it was *that* woman the dragon furiously sought to destroy.

I have been to the Piedmont mountains of northwest Italy, and there on the mountainsides, in the cloistered valleys, I have stood with a reverent hush in the same rocky caves and Alpine hideouts where the hunted Waldenses once huddled, that beleaguered community of faithful men, women, and children that defied Rome. Pursued by the bloodthirsty prostitute with her armies, the prophetic woman in hiding was no apocalyptic myth. She was the bride of Christ hunted like an animal and cut down wherever her faithful, loyal children were discovered through those long, dark Middle Ages.

> When the dragon saw that he had been hurled to the earth, he pursued the woman who had given birth to the male child. The woman was given the two wings of a great eagle, so that she might fly to the place prepared for her in the wilderness, where she would be taken care of for a time, times and half a time [3½ prophetic years = 1,260 prophetic days = 1,260 actual years], out of the serpent's reach. Then from his mouth the serpent spewed water like a river, to overtake the woman and sweep her away with the torrent (Revelation 12:13–15).

During those 1,260 years, the dragon's roar echoed from the snow-clad mountain peaks as the dark, bloody reign of the prostitute woman, the counterfeit church, marched wave after wave of weaponized attackers into those valleys to hunt the Vaudois, or Waldenses, believers. All the victims pleaded for was the right to follow Holy Scripture and worship their Creator according to the dictates of their own consciences. But the dragon, twice humiliated—by his expulsion from heaven and then by his devasting defeat at Calvary—would brook no comprise.

Standing on the edge of the famed Castelluzzo mountain cliff in northwest Italy, I looked over that precipice from where men, women, and children were hurled to their deaths hundreds of feet below. The butchery that invaded the Waldenses' cloistered communities is too graphic to detail here. J. A. Wylie, in his *History of the Waldenses*, defers: "These cruelties form a scene that is unparalleled and unique in the history of at least civilized countries. There have been tragedies in which more blood was spilled, and more life sacrificed, but none in which the actors were so completely dehumanized, and the forms of suffering so monstrously disgusting, so unutterably cruel and revolting. The Piedmontese massacres [in April 1655] in this respect stand alone."[9]

The English poet John Milton (1608–1674), upon learning of the extermination of so many fellow Protestants, wrote his epic sonnet "On the Late Massacre in Piedmont." Here are a handful of lines from his lament:

> Avenge, O Lord, thy slaughtered saints, whose bones
> Lie scattered on the Alpine mountains cold,

> Even them who kept thy truth so pure of old,
> When all our fathers worshiped stocks and stones.[10]

And let us not conclude the woman in hiding from the bloodthirsty dragon was confined to the Piedmont mountains of Italy. In France a century earlier, the Saint Bartholomew's Day massacre (August 24–25, 1572) became one of the bloodiest attempts ever at exterminating the truth as it is in Jesus. In a single night, thousands of French Huguenots (descendants of the Waldenses faith) were slaughtered. The truth of both history and prophecy is that the 1,260 years were long, dark, and blood-soaked: "The history of the medieval church leaves behind the bloody trail of the Crusades, of the Inquisition, of the massacres of Saint Bartholomew's Day, and of the Thirty Years' War. Thousands of victims—Protestants, Huguenots, Jews, even Catholics—preferred to shed their own blood rather than submit unthinkingly to the politico-religious institution."[11]

> But blackest in the black catalogue of crime, most horrible among the fiendish deeds of all the dreadful centuries [of the Dark Ages], was the St. Bartholomew Massacre. The world still recalls with shuddering horror the scenes of that most cowardly and cruel onslaught. . . .
> . . . Neither age nor sex was respected. Neither the innocent babe nor the man of gray hairs was spared. Noble and peasant, old and young, mother and child, were cut down together. Throughout France the butchery continued for two months. Seventy thousand of the very flower of the nation perished.[12]

John describes the whore this way:

> I saw that the woman was drunk with the blood of God's holy people, the blood of those who bore testimony to Jesus.
> When I saw her, I was greatly astonished (Revelation 17:6).

But just when it appears the dragon through his surrogate whore has the woman, the pure bride of Christ, cornered and at last can move in for the kill, history dramatically swerves, and the woman is delivered.

"But the earth helped the woman by opening its mouth and swallowing the river that the dragon had spewed out of his mouth" (Revelation 12:16).

Two dramatic events at the end of the Middle Ages bring deliverance to the woman. The titular head of the Middle Ages' ruling church was taken captive in 1798 by order of Napoleon, effectively hobbling her reach and influence. Doukhan illumines the event: "The French Revolution would confront the church with an atheistic society having but one god: reason. But most important, in 1798 the French army under the commanding office of General Berthier would invade Rome, capture the pope, and deport him. General Bonaparte intended to eradicate papal and church authority. Ironically, it was France, the 'eldest daughter of the Church,' who had originally established the papacy as a political power. Now the nation would strip the pope of his prerogatives."[13]

At the same time across the stormy Atlantic, a new nation was birthed out of the barren wilderness of the New World, a land that threw wide its doors to the downtrodden and persecuted masses of Europe.

"But the earth helped the woman." Recall the earth beast, the apocalyptic symbol in Revelation 13 we examined earlier—that land divinely raised up to become a safe haven far away from the crowded thoroughfares of Europe at the end of the 1700s, a nation that would one day become a global superpower, a new land where the woman and her children might grow up unmolested and free in the truth as it is in Jesus.

You mean America was raised up to become a safe haven for the persecuted in Europe?

Yes. I believe the fledgling New World was co-opted by God to become a refuge for those fleeing the church of the Old World? "[In America] it was demonstrated that the principles of the Bible are the surest safeguards of national greatness . . . and the world marked with wonder the peace and prosperity of 'a church without a pope, and a state without a king.' "[14]

The Apocalypse is clear. Heaven sought a safe haven within which the woman could birth her remnant, her end-time children—a home base, as it were, from which the woman's remnant children could launch their global mission in preparation for the endgame between the dragon and Christ our Lord.

"And the dragon was enraged with the woman, and he went to make war with the rest ["remnant" in the KJV] of her offspring, who keep the commandments of God and have the testimony of Jesus Christ" (Revelation 12:17, NKJV).

There it is—the remnant church—or simply the bride of Christ at the end of time. And how are these people making up the remnant described? They "keep the commandments of God and have the testimony of Jesus."

Whatever else they may be, like the dragon-hunted faithful through the centuries of spiritual warfare and cosmic conflict, they will live radically obediently to God's commandments, embracing the truth as it is in Jesus, no matter the crimson price such loyalty exacts. "They did not love their lives so much as to shrink from death" (Revelation 12:11).

Whoever they are, they are a Jesus people—these remnant, endgame children of the bride of Christ. And their testimony about Him cannot be controverted. Plain and simple: Jesus is the Lord of salvation (Matthew 11:28), and He is the Lord of the Sabbath (Mark 2:28). Thus the woman of the Apocalypse has always been Sabbatarian, both before and after the birth of the Messiah. For she has always defended the authority of God's law, the Ten Commandments, and the lordship of the Creator through His seventh-day Sabbath (Genesis 2:1–3; Exodus 20:11). Whatever the New Testament church championed, she has kept on championing. Thus, for two thousand years, the woman, hated by the dragon but beloved of heaven, has proclaimed the everlasting gospel and the truth as it is in Jesus (Revelation 14:6). It is no wonder the dragon has singled her out for his most venomous rage!

Jacques Doukhan summarizes the twin markers of this end-time faith community: "The remnant is characterized by its obedience and faithfulness—they 'obey.' They have not lost what God has entrusted them with. Furthermore they are the last witnesses to a truth that comprehends all opposites, transcends all factions. It is a truth that appreciates the Torah [law] of the Jews along with the Yeshua [Jesus] of the Christians, bringing together grace and law, love and justice, creation and judgment, and the New and Old Testaments. This truth combines 'God's commandments' with the 'testimony of Jesus' the Messiah (Rev. 12:17)."[15]

Some people say it really doesn't matter if you belong to the church, as long as you love Jesus. That would be like saying, "Jesus, I love You—I just can't stand Your bride." Would you ever dare say that to a husband? Not if you want to live to see tomorrow!

The Bible is clear that Christ is married to the church and the church to Him: "Christ loved the church and gave himself up for her to make her holy, cleansing her by the washing with water through the word, and to present her to himself as a radiant church, without stain or wrinkle or any other blemish, but holy and blameless" (Ephesians 5:25–27). When you connect with Christ, you join His bride. When you disconnect with His bride, you disconnect from Him. Ipso facto that is divine truth, which explains why the dragon, with such hot-breathed vehemence, seeks to keep you disconnected from either Christ or His bride. It doesn't matter which one, because when you disconnect from one, you disconnect from the other. And either way, the dragon has you.

But the good news of all of this is embedded in Jesus' provocative words to Saul on the Damascus road: "I am Jesus, whom you are persecuting" (Acts 9:5). You can't get any closer than that! So with the forces in heaven and on Earth now intensifying for the final battle, does it not make logical sense that *today is the right day to decide for Jesus and His church*? Who knows how much longer this earth beast—this New World land of liberty and freedom—can remain a divinely intended safe haven for the woman's end-time seed? We are running out of time. And so is America.

This much we can know: "God's love for His church is infinite."[16]

And if God so loves the church, shouldn't we so love her, too?

1. It is a story for another time—the son of American missionaries in Japan being rescued from beside a mountain lake by a United States Air Force helicopter and transported over the mountains to the distant air base hospital outside Tokyo, where he recovered (God be praised) in a room full of wounded American soldiers (from Vietnam), who loaded this American kid with comics, chewing gum, and candy.

2. Ellen G. White, *Testimonies to Ministers and Gospel Workers* (Mountain View, CA: Pacific Press®, 1962), 114.

3. If you're having a hard time visualizing the scene, go to Google and enter the terms *woman* and *seven-headed dragon* to see a score of artists' renditions.

4. Sigve Tonstad, *Revelation* (Grand Rapids, MI: Baker Academic, 2019), 176.

5. "Ask me, and I will make the nations your inheritance, the ends of the earth your possession. You will break them with a rod of iron; you will dash them to pieces like pottery" (Psalm 2:8, 9).

6. Tonstad, *Revelation*, 177.

7. The times are equal because the Bible reckons time based on the Hebrew thirty-day month and 360-day year: 1,260 days divided by 30 is 42 months.

8. 3½ years x 30 = 1,260 days ÷ 30 = 42 months.

9. J. A. Wylie, *History of the Waldenses* (Mountain View, CA: Pacific Press®, 1977), 142.

10. Wikipedia, s.v. "On the Last Massacre in Piedmont," last modified March 10, 2021, https://en.wikipedia.org/wiki/On_the_Late_Massacre_in_Piedmont.

11. Jacques Doukhan, *Secrets of Daniel: Wisdom and Dreams of a Jewish Prince* (Hagerstown, MD: Review and Herald®, 2000), 109.

12. Ellen G. White, *The Great Controversy* (Mountain View, CA: Pacific Press®, 1950), 272.

13. Doukhan, *Secrets of Daniel*, 109, 110.

14. White, *Great Controversy*, 296.

15. Jacques Doukhan, *Secrets of Revelation: The Apocalypse Through Hebrew Eyes* (Hagerstown, MD: Review and Herald®, 2002), 112.

16. Ellen G. White, *Testimonies for the Church*, vol. 9 (Mountain View, CA: Pacific Press®, 1948), 228.

Perhaps instead of asking the question, "Is America under divine judgment?" we ought to wonder aloud, "Will America *come under* divine judgment?"

"CALAMITIES MOST AWFUL, MOST UNEXPECTED"

Is America under judgment, divine judgment? "My country, 'tis of thee, sweet land of liberty, of thee I sing."[1] I'm wondering about *that* America. Is this pandemic perhaps an expression of divine displeasure with this nation?

Say what you will about the pandemic; on this, we can all agree: the COVID-19 coronavirus nearly single-handedly upended not only this nation but the entire planet overnight! In a matter of days, civilization was locked down, borders were sealed, economies collapsed as tens of thousands began to die of a mysterious killer virus for which there seemed no effective medical intervention. Even the frontline medical workers were succumbing. Humans cried out to their gods for deliverance. But the death toll kept climbing.

Those two critical points—"in a matter of days" and "the entire planet"—are worth repeating, given our short-term memory limitation as human beings. Even the Bible is quick to finger our forgetfulness: "Above all, you must understand that in the last days scoffers will come, scoffing and following their own evil desires. They will say, 'Where is this "coming" he promised? Ever since our ancestors died, everything goes on as it has since the beginning of creation' " (2 Peter 3:3, 4). Oh, really? Then what about the Flood? Beware the notion that Earth and homeostasis can endlessly ramble along. The pandemic has certainly diminished the numbers of those who lull themselves to sleep with the bromide "This too shall pass."

While we have perhaps weathered the worst of the pandemic now, America—with the largest death toll on this planet, heading toward one million deaths—is struggling to return to some sort of normalcy. But the "new normal" has hardly assuaged our fears or calmed our angst. Our troubling questions for the future and the next cataclysm are short and sweet: When, where, and how?

Was this pandemic sent from God to punish America? Cliff Goldstein, in a piece titled "Avert Judgement? On God's Wrath Being Poured Out on America," considers the question. First, he quotes Abraham Lincoln, warning about slavery in his second inaugural address: "Fondly do we hope, fervently do we pray, that this mighty scourge of war [the Civil War] may speedily pass away. Yet, if God wills that it continue until all the wealth piled by the bondsman's two hundred and fifty years of unrequited toil shall be sunk, and until every drop of blood drawn with the lash shall be paid by another drawn with the sword, as was said three thousand years ago, so still it must be said 'the judgments of the Lord are true and righteous altogether.' "[2]

Is America under divine judgment? Some think so. Goldstein recalls that soon after the Twin Towers terrorist attacks on September 11, 2001, "the late Reverend Jerry Falwell opined that God had allowed the attacks because the United States had become a land of 'pagans, abortionists, feminists, gays, lesbians, the American Civil Liberties Union and the People for the American Way.' "[3] (Goldstein notes Falwell later apologized to gays and lesbians.)

Albert Mohler, who at that time was president of the Southern Baptist Theological Seminary and still is at the time of this writing, commented on Jerry Falwell's indictment: "There is no doubt that America has accommodated itself to so many sins that we should always fear God's judgment and expect that in due time that judgment will come. But we ought to be very careful about pointing to any circumstance or any specific tragedy and say that this thing has happened because this is God's direct punishment."[4]

Wise counsel. Perhaps instead of asking the question, "Is America under divine judgment?" we ought to wonder aloud, "Will America *come under* divine judgment?"

Consider the doom-and-gloom warning issued by Ezekiel, a young prophet in exile. One cannot help conjecturing if this warning to Israel is apropos for America, too:

> The word of the LORD came to me: "Son of man, this is what the Sovereign LORD says to the land of Israel:
>
> 'The end! The end has come
>   upon the four corners of the land!
> The end is now upon you,

and I will unleash my anger against you.
I will judge you according to your conduct
and repay you for all your detestable practices' " (Ezekiel 7:1–3).

Apparently, an entire nation can come under divine judgment:

This is what the Sovereign LORD says:
"Disaster! Unheard-of disaster!
See, it comes!
The end has come!
The end has come!
It has roused itself against you.
See, it comes" (Ezekiel 7:5, 6).

Did you count the exclamation marks?

Every hand will go limp;
every leg will be wet with urine [a graphic depiction of a
physiological response to fear].
They will put on sackcloth
and be clothed with terror.
Every face will be covered with shame,
and every head will be shaved.

They will throw their silver into the streets,
and their gold will be treated as a thing unclean.
Their silver and gold
will not be able to deliver them
in the day of the LORD's wrath.
It will not satisfy their hunger
or fill their stomachs,
for it has caused them to stumble into sin (Ezekiel 7:17–19).

Calamity strikes the hapless nation! But the prophet goes on.

When terror [a word our generation knows all too well] comes,
they will seek peace in vain.
Calamity upon calamity will come,
and rumor upon rumor.

They will go searching for a vision from the prophet,
    priestly instruction in the law will cease,
    the counsel of the elders will come to an end.
The king [the highest political office in the land] will mourn,
    the prince will be clothed with despair,
    and the hands of the people of the land will tremble [they will
      experience uncontrolled fear].
I will deal with them according to their conduct,
    and by their own standards I will judge them (Ezekiel 7:25–27).

There it is, that notion of judgment. Could it be that the calamities and terror that once descended upon ancient Israel in some way foreshadow a calamity this nation and world have yet to face?

Just as somber is the warning from the nineteenth-century writer Ellen White: "Transgression has almost reached its limit. Confusion fills the world, and a great terror is soon to come upon human beings. The end is very near. We who know the truth should be preparing for what is soon to break upon the world as an overwhelming surprise."[5]

Ezekiel's prediction that "calamity upon calamity will come . . . and the hands of the people of the land will tremble" is echoed by White's statements that "a great terror is soon to come upon human beings" and that "we . . . should be preparing for what is soon to break upon the world as an overwhelming surprise."

But what compounds these forewarnings is the sobering reality that Jesus Himself issued a nearly identical warning. Consider these words of His that we may have read before, but perhaps their grave import we have never really quite grasped. Describing events in the natural world that would be harbingers of His second coming, Jesus predicted: "There will be signs in the sun, moon and stars. On the earth, nations will be in anguish and perplexity at the roaring and tossing of the sea. People will faint from terror, apprehensive of what is coming on the world, for the heavenly bodies will be shaken. At that time they will see the Son of Man coming in a cloud with power and great glory" (Luke 21:25–27). Talk about a red-letter warning!

Jesus begins with the heavenly bodies—"the sun, moon and stars"—and then seems to diverge to the "roaring and tossing of the sea." After which He returns to the heavenly bodies with the prediction that "they will be shaken." And as a consequence of whatever He is predicting will transpire, He describes the inhabitants of this planet (not just this nation) thrown into deep "anguish and perplexity." So what is going on? What is Jesus predicting?

Some years ago, I read an unpublished paper by writer and editor Marvin Moore, which helped me discern in this red-letter warning from Jesus the possibility of a prediction I had never seen before. Moore subsequently published his research in his book *The Coming Great Calamity*, to which I am indebted.[6]

Notice how Marvin Moore parses these two words of Jesus, "anguish and perplexity:" *anguish* can mean "This hurts a lot" or "This is terrible," and *perplexity* means "What do we do now?" He graphically describes the phrase: "Anguish and perplexity is what you would feel if you were to come home one night and find your house in flames."[7] That is, "This hurts a lot—so what do we do now?"

The point is well taken because when members of my own faith community read Jesus' prediction of signs in the sun, moon, and stars (as we just did), we review historical celestial events that we correctly believe ushered in the great prophetic period of Bible prophecy called "the time of the end" (as Daniel, Jesus, and John in Revelation described it). In the Apocalypse, John described such celestial events: "I watched as he opened the sixth seal. There was a great earthquake. The sun turned black like sackcloth made of goat hair, the whole moon turned blood red, and the stars in the sky fell to earth, as figs drop from a fig tree when shaken by a strong wind" (Revelation 6:12, 13). Students of Bible prophecy have identified historically significant and documented events in the heavens as harbingers of the end—for example, the falling of the stars[8] and the Dark Day[9] with its subsequent moon turning blood red.[10]

But none of those celestial signs elicited the *global* (key word) reaction Jesus described as "anguish and perplexity"—that is, "This is terrible, so what do we do now?" Whatever the celestial event Jesus is predicting, He is clear about the universal response to it: "People will faint from terror, apprehensive of what is coming on the world, for the heavenly bodies will be shaken" (Luke 21:26).

Evidently, this unnamed event is so terribly unnatural and unexpected,

> Evidently, this unnamed event is so terribly unnatural and unexpected, so devastatingly cataclysmic, that the entire planet is paralyzed.

so devastatingly cataclysmic, that the entire planet is paralyzed. Because of "the heavenly bodies [being] shaken," society will be thrown into global panic. So what celestial sign could possibly elicit such a worldwide response? What is this universal calamity that is to occur, not at the beginning but rather at the end of that time-of-the-end prophetic period just before Christ returns to Earth?

Consider this possibility.

"In 1998 the U.S. Congress directed NASA to initiate what they called SpaceGuard, an effort to find and track 90% of all near-Earth objects 1 kilometer and larger [mass-extinction size] by 2008. In 2005, Congress expanded NASA's NEO [Near Earth Object] mandate to find and track at least 90% of all NEOs 140 meters or larger by 2020. . . . Only 40% of these objects have been found to date. At current detection rates, it will be another 30 years before NASA meets the goal."[11]

Asteroids—what everybody seems to be talking about these days. Have you noticed how frequently they appear in the news lately? Here is a random collection of online headlines appearing in the same month:

Asteroid twice as big as Empire State Building to fly past Earth next week.

> NASA said the asteroid is between 350 and 780 meters in diameter. Even at the lower end of this estimate, 1999 RM45 will be almost as tall as the Eiffel Tower in Paris, France. When the space rock passes by the Earth, scientists think it will be traveling at around 44,700 miles per hour—about 50 times faster than a handgun bullet. Due to close passes such as this, and others predicted in the future, NASA has classified 1999 RM45 as "potentially hazardous."[12]

An asteroid the size of the Golden Gate Bridge will pass by Earth in March.

> To make 2021 stand out even more, an asteroid as wide as the Golden Gate Bridge is scheduled to zoom past Earth next month. . . . This particular asteroid . . . is about 0.5 to 1 mile (0.8 to 1.7 kilometers) in diameter. It will, however, come within 2 million kilometers of our planet, raising a

red flag, according to a database published by NASA's Jet Propulsion Laboratory. The sheer size and range within Earth is enough to classify it as "potentially hazardous."[13]

3 massive asteroids will zoom by Earth on Saturday.

> While NASA's Perseverance rover has arrived on Mars, three massive asteroids are currently heading toward Earth's vicinity and are expected to whiz past the planet this weekend. The near-Earth asteroids (NEA), identified as 2021 CU3, 2021 CC2 and 2021 CR3, are estimated to be around the size of or larger than the Great Pyramid of Giza in Egypt. . . . The [2021 CU3] asteroid will also be the fastest-moving among the three as it is currently hurtling through space at an average velocity of 58,000 miles per hour (93,000 kilometers per hour).[14]

What's the big deal, and why are Congress and NASA so earnest about tracking these roving and rogue space rocks? Keep reading.

For me, the paradigm shift regarding asteroids occurred on a Friday morning, February 15, 2013. I was in my study when I heard the news about an explosion near the Russian city of Chelyabinsk. Eyewitness news accounts reported a streaking asteroid, captured on multiple dashcam videos, entering our atmosphere at 40,000–42,900 MPH. It was only 20 meters long, the size of a large school bus. But it exploded with a blast yield of 400–500 kilotons of TNT, which is thirty times the energy of the atomic bomb at Hiroshima. The detonating asteroid shattered windows, damaged buildings, and injured more than a thousand people. Fortunately, nobody was killed.[15]

Asteroids—what everybody seems to be talking about these days. Have you noticed how frequently they appear in the news lately?

About a hundred years earlier, in eastern Siberia, on June 30, 1908, what is now known as the Tunguska asteroid (estimated to be perhaps 65 meters in length) exploded in the atmosphere with a 15-megaton blast, one thousand times the energy of Hiroshima's atomic bomb. That nuclear-like detonation flattened an uninhabited forest of eighty million trees over 830 square miles of eastern Siberia.[16]

Consider these two salient facts concerning these two over-Russia asteroids. First, they were too small (20 meters and 65 meters) to be on anybody's radar screen since both NASA and the European Space Agency are searching for asteroids 140 meters and larger.

Second, look at the damage these small asteroids inflicted. If a Tunguska-sized asteroid hit a typical rural portion of the United States, it is estimated seventy thousand people would be killed with billions of dollars of losses in property damage. But if a Tunguska-sized asteroid struck an urban area, the death toll would climb to three hundred thousand and the loss of property in the hundreds of billions of dollars.[17]

> In reality, all it would take to fulfill Jesus' startling prophecy of global panic is a single celestial event, a devastating nuclear-like hit from outer space. Talk about "the powers of the heavens will be shaken" (Luke 21:26, NKJV)!

Nevertheless, astronomers now estimate there are two million 30-meter and larger asteroids in our solar system, with only eighteen thousand of them thus far identified! By the way, the only way you can identify an asteroid is by optical lens—not by radar. You have to see them to know they are there. For that reason, NASA has designed its Near-Earth Object Surveillance Mission space-based infrared telescope to search our solar system for potentially hazardous, heretofore unidentified flying objects.

And one more caveat. If an asteroid comes from out of the sun toward us, it cannot be seen at all! The closest near miss we have ever experienced occurred August 16, 2020, when Asteroid 2020 QG—flying at 7.7 miles per second—approached Earth from a sunward direction and blew past us at 4:08 UT (11:08 p.m. EsT). It was only 1,831 miles from us! In fact, it got so close to us, Earth's gravity actually bent the asteroid's trajectory. And guess what? We learned of it six hours *after* it blew by. The sobering point? Just a few decimal points' difference in that asteroid's trajectory, and the blow-by could have been a cataclysmic blowup.

But none of this is rocket science. There is an organization of scientists called the B612 Foundation. Attributed to them is this cheery factoid: "It's 100 per cent certain we'll be hit by a [devastating asteroid], but we're not a 100 per cent sure when."[18] Isn't that helpful!

In reality, all it would take to fulfill Jesus' startling prophecy of global panic is a single celestial event, a devastating nuclear-like hit from outer space. Talk about "the powers of the heavens will be shaken" (Luke 21:26, NKJV)! One asteroid, undetected until too late or perhaps never detected at all, slamming into this terrestrial ball that is home sweet home to us all—you don't need Hollywood special effects to portray the outcome. In fact, a tidal wave strike in the Gulf of Mexico from an extinction-event size asteroid would create a wall of water—by some estimates up to 5 kilometers high—that would still be racing at 457 meters high 900 miles from the impact! That tidal wave would not only wipe out coastal regions and populations but it would also flood Kansas City![19] "For the heavenly bodies will be shaken."

Read it again, Jesus' endgame warning: "There will be signs in the sun, moon and stars. On the earth, nations will be in anguish and perplexity at the roaring and tossing of the sea. People will faint from terror, apprehensive of what is coming on the world, for the heavenly bodies will be shaken. At that time they will see the Son of Man coming in a cloud with power and great glory" (Luke 21:25–27). His words suddenly take on a much more urgent meaning, do they not?

"Transgression has almost reached its limit. Confusion fills the world, and *a great terror is soon to come upon human beings*. The end is very near. We who know the truth should be preparing for what is soon to break upon the world as an overwhelming surprise."[20]

"What are you trying to do—scare me?" No. But in all candor, I am earnestly hoping you and I will wake up. Do you remember when we used to stay in hotels? (Thanks to this pandemic, it has been a while.) How many times—when you had an early morning flight to catch back home (it's the back-home flights you never want to miss)—have you called the front desk to request a wake-up call? Yes, you have your alarm set. But to make sure you don't sleep through the alarm, you order a wake-up call.

I believe what is transpiring on Earth right now is a huge wake-up call. It brings God no joy to watch the suffering this pandemic has inflicted upon the earth. Jesus was very clear in His attribution of blame when he said, "An enemy has done this" (Matthew 13:28, NKJV). Heaven grieves the suffering that continues unabated on this planet. There is no joy over the raging wildfires that have swept entire communities off the map; no joy over the destroying hurricane winds and floodwaters that wipe out neighborhoods in my own region of the country. So be assured it would give God no joy for an errant asteroid to break through our atmosphere and strike a populated city or region one day.

But if our lethargy is of such a degree that we are ignoring or missing the mounting evidences of Jesus' soon return, then a desperate Love has no recourse but to pound on the door of a civilization rapidly being engulfed in flames—*before* it is too late. C. S. Lewis was right: "God whispers to us in our pleasures, speaks in our conscience, but shouts in our pain: it is His megaphone to rouse a deaf world."[21]

Ellen White concurs: "Calamities will come—calamities most awful, most unexpected; and these destructions will follow one after another. If there will be a heeding of the warnings that God has given . . . then other cities may be spared for a time. . . . God allows them to suffer calamity [as Lewis wrote, "His megaphone to rouse a deaf world"], that their senses may be awakened."[22]

Paul issues the same warning: "For you yourselves know perfectly that the day of the Lord so comes as a thief in the night. For when they say, 'Peace and safety!' then *sudden destruction* comes upon them, as labor pains upon a pregnant woman. And they shall not [in the Greek this is a double negative: "No not ever"] escape" (1 Thessalonians 5:2, 3, NKJV; emphasis added).

No wonder this six-word prayer: "God of heaven, wake us up!"[23]

But a wake-up call is not a call to fear. It is a call to faith and even hope. Just look at the promise Jesus made on the heels of His red-letter warning! Yes, His warning is clear: "People will faint from terror, apprehensive of what is coming on the world, for the heavenly bodies will be shaken" (Luke 21:26). But now read His hopeful promise: "At that time they will see the Son of Man coming in a cloud with power and great glory. When these things begin to take place, stand up and lift up your heads, because your redemption is drawing near" (Luke 21:27, 28). No call for fear here! Instead, Jesus' assurance is inescapable—on the heels of this unnamed calamity comes the ringing promise of His imminent return. And what should be the posture of His friends who await Him? No head-down, heart-in-your-throat fear for them. Just the opposite, in fact: Stand up! Lift up your heads! For your deliverance is on the way! Can you think of any better news for a planet in crisis?

Why even the psalmist concurs:

God is our refuge and strength,
A very present help in trouble.
Therefore we will not fear,
Even though the earth be removed,
And though the mountains be carried into the midst of the sea [effects
of an earthquake or asteroid];
Though its waters roar and be troubled [effects of a tsunami],
Though the mountains shake with its swelling. . . .
The LORD of hosts is with us;
The God of Jacob is our refuge (Psalm 46:1–3, 11, NKJV).

Good news! God is with us no matter what lies ahead in this planet's upheavals, in America's gathering gloom. "Therefore we will not fear."

One night during the height of the blitzkrieg over London during World War II, a father and his little girl fled to their backyard underground shelter for safety. It was apparent the two of them must spend the night in that small dark cubicle. Above them were death and destruction. Panic ruled the night, and the little girl was scared.

Father tucked her into one of the small cots in that shelter, then turned out the light and lay down on the cot against the other wall. But the girl couldn't sleep. The rumble overhead, the strangeness of an underground room she had never been in before, and the black shadows filled her with fear. Her mommy was gone. And she knew that above her in the night, many were dying. In the darkness, she felt desperately alone.

She didn't cry, but as the minutes ticked by, she couldn't stand it any longer, and she whispered across the dark space, "Daddy, are you there?"

"Yes, dear, I'm here; now go to sleep," was his quiet response.

She tried, but she just couldn't. And before long, that tiny voice spoke again, "Daddy, are you *still* there?"

Quick was his answer, "Yes, darling, I'm here. Don't be afraid, just go to sleep. It's all right." And for some time, there was only silence, each lost in his or her own thoughts.

But finally, when the stillness and darkness were no longer bearable, the voice of the little one, craving assurance, spoke the third time. "Daddy," she called out, "please tell me just one thing more: *Is your face turned this way?*"

And through the dark quickly came the voice of her father in reply, "Yes, darling, Daddy is right here, and his face is turned your way." In an instant, the little girl fell asleep in the perfect trust of a little child.[24]

"God is our refuge and strength, a very present help in trouble. Therefore we will not fear" (Psalm 46:1, 2, NRSV). Just the news we need, we who live in these dark hours of uncertainty: The face of our Father is turned our way. We have nothing to fear.

---

1. Samuel Francis Smith, "My Country 'Tis of Thee" (1832).

2. Abraham Lincoln, quoted in Cliff Goldstein, "Avert Judgment? On God's Wrath Being Poured Out on America," *Liberty*, July/August 2020, 6.

3. Goldstein.

4. Albert Mohler, quoted in Goldstein, "Avert Judgment?," 7.

5. Ellen G. White, *Testimonies for the Church*, vol. 8 (Mountain View, CA: Pacific Press®, 1948), 28.

6. Marvin Moore, *The Coming Great Calamity* (Boise, ID: Pacific Press®, 1997).

7. Moore, 42.

8. " 'On the night of November 12th to 13th, 1833,' wrote Victorian astronomy writer Agnes Clerke, 'a tempest of falling stars broke over the Earth. The sky was scored in every direction with shining tracks and illuminated with majestic fireballs. At Boston, the frequency of meteors was estimated to be about half that of flakes of snow in an average snowstorm. Their numbers . . . were quite beyond counting; but as it waned, a reckoning was attempted, from which it was computed, on the basis of that much-diminished rate, that 240,000 must have been visible during the nine hours they continued to fall.' " Donal O'Keeffe, " 'They Thought It Was Judgment Day': The Night the Stars Fell on the US South," *Irish Times*, November 11, 2019, https://www.irishtimes.com/culture/they-thought-it-was-judgment-day-the-night-the-stars-fell-on-the-us-south-1.4075652.

9. "New England's Dark Day occurred on May 19, 1780, when an unusual darkening of the daytime sky was observed over the New England states and parts of Canada. The primary cause of the event is believed to have been a combination of smoke from forest fires, a thick fog, and cloud cover. The darkness was so complete that candles were required from noon on. It did not disperse until the middle of the next night." Wikipedia, s.v. "New England's Dark Day," last modified April 26, 2021, https://en.wikipedia.org/wiki/New_England%27s_Dark_Day.

10. "The sun will be turned to darkness and the moon to blood before the coming of the great and dreadful day of the LORD" (Joel 2:31).

11. Jason Davis, "Planetary Society Grant Winner Discovers Large Near-Earth Asteroid," Planetary Society, September 10, 2020, https://www.planetary.org/articles/planetary-society-grant-winner-discovers-large-asteroid.

12. Ed Browne, "Asteroid Twice as Big as Empire State Building to Fly Past Earth Next Week," *Newsweek*, February 23, 2021, https://www.newsweek.com/nasa-asteroid-1999rm45-close-pass-earth-empire-state-building-1571285.

13. Sonia Ramirez, "An Asteroid the Size of the Golden Gate Bridge Will Pass by Earth in March," Chron., February 23, 2021, https://www.chron.com/news/space/article/Golden-Gate-Bridge-size-asteroid-pass-Earth-15972211.php.

14. Alexis Ty, "3 Massive Asteroids Will Zoom by Earth on Saturday," International Business Times, February 19, 2021, https://www.ibtimes.com/3-massive-asteroids-will-zoom-earth-saturday-3148288.

15. Wikipedia, s.v. "Chelyabinsk Meteor," last modified May 30, 2021, https://en.wikipedia.org/wiki/Chelyabinsk_meteor.

16. Wikipedia, s.v. "Tunguska Event," last modified May 14, 2021, https://en.wikipedia.org/wiki/Tunguska_event.

17. Moore, *Coming Great Calamity*, 50.

18. Wikipedia, s.v. "B612 Foundation," last modified May 22, 2021, https://en.wikipedia.org/wiki/B612_Foundation.

19. Moore, *Coming Great Calamity*, 53.

20. White, *Testimonies for the Church*, 8:28; emphasis added.

21. C. S. Lewis, *The Problem of Pain*, reprint ed. (San Francisco: HarperSanFrancisco, 2001), 91, quoted in Jana Harmon, "C. S. Lewis on the Problem of Pain," C. S. Lewis Institute, August 12, 2012, https://www.cslewisinstitute.org/C_S_Lewis_on_the_Problem_of_Pain_page4.

22. Ellen G. White, *Maranatha* (Washington, DC: Review and Herald®, 1976), 176.

23. Ellen G. White, *Last Day Events* (Boise, ID: Pacific Press®, 1992), 27.

24. Llewellyn A. Wilcox, *Now Is the Time* (Escondido, CA: Outdoor Pictures, 1966), 129.

When the president of the United States

holds high a Bible in front of a shuttered

church during a pandemic for a photo

op, the cameras may be in focus, but the

separation between the state and religion

is certainly blurred.

BLUE LAWS AND
THE LAW-AND-ORDER PLATFORM

Would you like to see a side of America we never dreamed possible? Have you ever heard of blue laws? What are they?

Blue laws, also known as Sunday laws, are laws designed to restrict or ban some or all Sunday activities for religious or secular reasons, particularly to promote the observance of a day of worship or rest. Blue laws may also restrict shopping or ban sale of certain items on specific days, most often on Sundays in the western world. Blue laws are enforced in parts of the United States and Canada as well as some European countries, particularly in Austria, Germany, Switzerland, and Norway, keeping most stores closed on Sundays."[1]

Yes, but as far as the United States is concerned, hasn't the Supreme Court pretty much negated these blue law vestiges of old America? Yes and no:

The Supreme Court of the United States held in its landmark case, *McGowan v. Maryland* (1961), that Maryland's blue laws violated neither the Free Exercise Clause nor the Establishment Clause ["Congress shall make no law respecting an establishment of religion, or prohibiting the free exercise thereof"] of the First Amendment to the United States Constitution. It approved the state's blue law restricting commercial activities on Sunday, noting that while such laws originated to encourage attendance at Christian churches, the contemporary Maryland laws were intended to serve "to provide a uniform day of rest for all citizens" on a secular basis and to promote the secular values of "health, safety, recreation, and general well-being" through a common day of rest. That this day coincides with Christian Sabbath is not a bar to the state's secular goals; it neither reduces its effectiveness for secular purposes nor prevents adherents of other religions from observing their own holy days.[2]

Yes, the First Amendment of the Constitution both forbids the establishment of religion by the state and protects the free exercise of religion by the individual. But in this season of the pandemic in America, where social practice and legal parameters face mounting challenges, all ostensibly in the name of civil protection and the preservation of our security and safety, the line between free exercise and establishment can be blurred. When the president of the United States holds high a Bible in front of a shuttered church during a pandemic for a photo op, the cameras may be in focus, but the separation between the state and religion is certainly blurred.

So when politicians campaign on a law-and-order platform, it is fair to wonder whose law and whose order are advocated. Is anybody interested in advocating God's law?

On Christmas Eve 1968, the three astronauts aboard Apollo 8 looked down on our blue-green terrestrial ball and took turns reading the first ten verses of Genesis chapter 1—to the largest television audience at that time in history.

"In the beginning God created the heavens and the earth. Now the earth was formless and empty, darkness was over the surface of the deep, and the Spirit of God was hovering over the waters" (Genesis 1:1, 2). These are arguably the most well-known words of ancient holy Scripture. They are the divine preamble to the account of Earth's creation in seven days.

One by one, six days pass before the eyes of the reader—evening and morning, evening and morning. And when at the end of the sixth day, the Creator surveys His fresh primordial garden planet, with a pride and joy every craftsman knows, He pronounces it all "very good" (Genesis 1:31).

But His Creation is not over, not yet:

> Thus the heavens and the earth were completed in all their vast array.
>
> By the seventh day God had finished the work he had been doing; so on the seventh day he rested from all his work. Then God blessed the seventh day and made it holy, because on it he rested from all the work of creating that he had done (Genesis 2:1–3).

George McCready Price, in his provocative book *Time of the End,* observes the following:

> From the beginning the Creator planned to have a memorial of His *method* of creating. It would be for the good and lasting happiness of mankind for them to remember His creatorship, His power, His sovereignty. He could have accomplished the making of the earth and its plants and animals in one day, or even instantaneously. But He did not. He might have prolonged this creative act for ten days, or thirty. But He did not. He deliberately planned to do it by stages, spread out over six days, with a special extra day at the close as an official memorial of what He had done and *how He had done it.*[3]

For those of us who have grown up with the Creation story, this is an intriguing thought. The Creator intended for His *method* of creation, not just the *fact* of it, to be kept front and center throughout all time.

Price goes on: "Then He put a perpetual blessing upon every succeeding seventh day as a holy day of rest, or ceasing from the divine activity of the work of creation. The mere fact of creation is important, but God thought that the *method* was also important and should be remembered."[4]

The seventh-day Sabbath has been in existence from the very first week of Earth's time. As Abraham Heschel described, "The seventh day is like a palace in time with a kingdom for all."[5] The Sabbath is "a palace in time" to flourish the Creator's forever friendship with His creation, His Earth children, every seventh day. Thus, the Sabbath is truly Love's gift, a gift of Himself. "See what great love the Father has lavished on us, that we should be called children of God!" (1 John 3:1).

Every seventh-day Sabbath announces these glad tidings. This means as long as Earth's Creator and His creation exist, so will the seventh-day Sabbath be a shining and most celebrative memorial. God and we are friends. Let it be repeated—in the gift of the Sabbath, God gives Himself.

No wonder the Sabbath is both the geometric and thematic, or literary, heart of God's Ten Commandments. Sigve Tonstad, in his book *The Lost Meaning of the Seventh Day,* describes the story embedded in the Sabbath: "The seventh day . . . is not willing to be estranged from its narratival roots. . . . The story of God's faithfulness that is etched in the seventh day . . . envisions a chain reaction of blessing, forging the Sabbath into a conduit of grace to all creation."[6]

For a moment, consider this narratival "conduit of grace" in two grand stories embedded in the Decalogue. Story no. 1—"I am the LORD your God, who brought you out of Egypt, out of the land of slavery" (Exodus 20:2).

Who doesn't thrill to the mighty retelling of the dramatic narrative of the exodus from Egypt! Wide-eyed children of all ages have watched the surround-sound saga of *The Prince of Egypt*—that gripping DreamWorks animation of Moses and the midnight deliverance of that nation of liberated slaves, saved by the blood of the Lamb, escorted by El Shaddai,[7] Almighty God Himself, who single-handedly through those ten plagues triumphed over every god and goddess in Egypt's pantheon of deities. It is truly one of the greatest stories of deliverance and redemption in all of human literature.

So the God who spoke the Ten Commandments into existence and then with His finger carved these ten precepts for human flourishing and happiness into granite[8]—before He spoke a single commandment, He first announced that the Giver of His Law is indeed the Deliverer of His people. "I am the LORD your God, who brought you out of Egypt, out of the land of slavery" (Exodus 20:2).

But God has another grand storied narrative embedded in the heart of the Ten Commandments, one that antedates the mighty Exodus by millennia.

Story no. 2: "Remember the Sabbath day by keeping it holy. Six days you shall labor and do all your work, but the seventh day is a sabbath to the LORD your God. On it you shall not do any work, neither you, nor your son or daughter, nor your male or female servant, nor your animals, nor any foreigner residing in your towns. For in six days the LORD made the heavens and the earth, the sea, and all that is in them, but he rested on the seventh day. Therefore the LORD blessed the Sabbath day and made it holy" (Exodus 20:8–11).

There it is—the ultimate story of humanity—the narrative of our creation at the hands of our Creator "in the beginning." To keep fresh in our minds and spirits both stories—the story of God as our Creator and the story of God as our Redeemer—every seventh day, God designed the Sabbath to be "a conduit of grace to all creation."[9]

The seventh-day Sabbath ignites a chain reaction of blessings. To quote Tonstad again: "The person who experiences God's faithfulness in the rest of the Sabbath is to extend the privilege to son and daughter, to male and female slave, to the resident alien, even to cattle . . . triggering an avalanche of blessing that is to make all Creation beneficiaries of the Sabbath."[10]

No wonder Jesus, the incarnated Creator of the universe,[11] was so big on the seventh-day Sabbath, "the palace in time"[12] He Himself had created into existence: "Then [Jesus] said to them, 'The Sabbath was made for man, not man for the Sabbath. So the Son of Man is Lord even of the Sabbath' " (Mark 2:27, 28).

There it is again, the Creator's gift of the Sabbath to humanity, the gift of Himself to the human race.

However, some Christians suggest that the Sabbath was made for the Jews and not for the rest of us. That is, when Jesus said, "The Sabbath was made for man," He really meant, "The Sabbath was made for the Jews." Oh really?

That is quite an intriguing thought, since the Creation story also reads, "And he [the Creator] brought her [the woman] to the man" (Genesis 2:22). If "the Sabbath was made for man" and that means only for the Jews, then does God's gift of woman to man mean only for the Jews as well? But of course not, or we would all be in trouble! Perhaps you respond, "Well, of course, woman wasn't made for Jews—there were no Jews back then."

And that is precisely the point. The Creator's gift of the seventh-day Sabbath was a gift to humanity for all time. So to suggest that Jesus, the incarnated Creator, meant that the Sabbath was made for Jews is simply wrongheaded. There were no Jews or Christians in the beginning. The gift of the Sabbath, Jesus informs His listeners, is a divine gift to humanity for all time.

Skip MacCarty, in the book *Perspectives on the Sabbath: Four Views*, writes in his opening extended essay: "When Mark recorded Jesus' words, 'the Sabbath was made for man' (2:27), he chose Greek terms that would communicate the universal and permanent character of the Sabbath. . . . The Greek term *anthropos* is the generic term for humankind. Numerous scholars have understood Mark 2:27 as Jesus' affirmation of the creation origin and universal character of the Sabbath."[13] In fact, J. H. Gerstner concludes: "In [Mark 2:27] that Christians commonly take today as liberating them from sabbatical law, Christ actually bound His followers more tightly to it."[14]

Why, Jesus' very use of Son of Man as a title for Himself further corroborates His universal appropriation and gift of the Sabbath to humanity. Noting that Mark quotes Jesus' self-designation as Son of Man fourteen times in his short gospel, MacCarty concludes:

By doing so, Jesus intended to convey that as He was the

Creator of all mankind, not of the Jews only, He was also the divine/human Savior of all mankind, not simply of the Jews. When Mark quoted Jesus' affirmation that "the Sabbath was made for man [*ton anthropon*, literally "the man"] (2:27), he likely had in mind both Genesis 1:27's revelation that "God created mankind" (literally "the man"), and Jesus' fourteen self-designations as "the Son of Man" (literally "the man"). *In other words, [even] as God created all humanity and Jesus came as Savior of all humanity, so the Sabbath was likewise made for all humanity.*[15]

What does this have to do with blue laws? To begin with, I am against Sunday blue laws as a means to solve our need for "law and order," simply because Jesus is Lord of the seventh-day Sabbath. And since He is, why should anybody seek to enforce the first day as the day of rest?

Then what shall we do with the Apocalypse's well-known and oft quoted sentence: "On the Lord's Day I was in the Spirit, and I heard behind me a loud voice like a trumpet" (Revelation 1:10).

"Aha!" you may exclaim. "There it is, Bible proof that Sunday became the Christians' new day of worship instead of the seventh-day Sabbath."

But just a minute. We need to be careful about jumping to conclusions. Think for a moment of the implications of that hurried assumption. Shall we, with that single phrase—"the Lord's Day"—wipe out the Creator's eternal memorial of His creatorship and friendship with humanity, as embedded in the seventh-day Sabbath? Shall we replace what He wrote with His finger in granite with our assumption that "the Lord's Day" means the first day of the week? Surely, you are not suggesting such, are you?

What day did you think Jesus is Lord of in the Bible? The fourth commandment of the Decalogue declares, "But the seventh day is the Sabbath of the LORD your God" (Exodus 20:10, NKJV). In the Ten Commandments, it is clear God is Lord of the seventh-day Sabbath. And that is precisely why, when the Creator became flesh and dwelt among us, He called the seventh-day Sabbath the day He is Lord of: "So the Son of Man is Lord even of the Sabbath" (Mark 2:28). Remember, the Jesus who wrote with His finger in the dust on the temple floor (John 8:6) is the same One who with His finger designated in granite the Sabbath as His day, the Lord's Day (Exodus 31:18).

Why, even the gospel prophet Isaiah declared the Sabbath to be the Lord's Day:

> If you call the Sabbath a delight
>> and *the* LORD'*s holy day* honorable,
> and if you honor it by not going your own way
>> and not doing as you please or speaking idle words,
> then you will find your joy in the LORD (Isaiah 58:13, 14; emphasis
> added).

Whether in the Old Testament or New Testament, the Bible plainly demarcates the seventh-day Sabbath as the Lord's Day of Scripture.

Jacques Doukhan, writing from a Hebrew perspective, confirms: "Yohanan [John] receives his vision on the 'Lord's Day' (Rev. 1:10). Most Christian readers think immediately of Sunday, forgetting that the writer is Jewish, nourished by the Hebrew Scriptures and steeped in the tradition of his ancestors."[16]

Then to elucidate the Bible Sabbath as the Lord's Day, he adds: "Moreover, history does not begin to refer to the 'Lord's Day' as Sunday until the second century C.E. Thus it is more plausible to think of the 'Lord's Day' as the Sabbath day, also called a day 'to the Lord' in the Hebrew Scriptures (Ex. 20:10; Deut. 5:14). Moreover, the frequent use of the number 7 in the Apocalypse justifies our allusion to the Sabbath day as the opening festival of the book."[17]

The Bible knows only one Lord's Day.[18]

Turning to history, MacCarty summarizes:

> Biblical evidence that the "Lord's Day" meant Sunday is entirely lacking. As does the rest of the NT, John in his own Gospel twice refers to Sunday as "the first day of the week," not the "Lord's Day." . . . The historical records reveal that the first unambiguous connection between "Lord's Day" and Sunday does not show up in Christian literature until the second half of the second century, many decades after John used the term. Therefore, it is clear that those who interpret the "Lord's Day" in Rev 1:10 as Sunday do this on the basis of extrabiblical evidence that is much later than the time when John wrote Revelation. This is an unsound methodology of biblical interpretation.[19]

Once again, the Lord's Day is clearly and biblically only one day—the seventh-day Sabbath. For it is the day our Lord Jesus is Lord of! He is both "Lord of the Sabbath" and "Lord of salvation." And that explains why on the seventh-day Sabbath (after Good Friday), the Lord of the Sabbath and salvation rested in the tomb after His crucifixion. As He had done at Creation, finishing His work and declaring it "very good" (Genesis 1:31), the same Creator and Savior, with that mighty cry "It is finished" brought completion to His work of redemption (John 19:30). *Then*, as it was in the beginning, He rested.

No wonder He calls humanity to *remember*. Because the truth is we have forgotten. "Remember the Sabbath day by keeping it holy" (Exodus 20:8).

When I was a boy growing up in Japan, I used to travel the trains to and from school every day during the busy rush hour. Packed like sardines? Like sardines on steroids! So I wasn't surprised to come across a news report of items Japanese train passengers had left on the trains over a twelve-month period. Guess how many umbrellas? Five hundred thousand. Cash? A total of $10.6 million (although 79 percent of it was later returned, obviously in wallets or purses). Included in the list of left-behind items were nine urns containing the ashes of loved ones. (That would be an embarrassing trip to the lost and found.)

The truth is, we humans are creatures of forgetfulness. So it should hardly be surprising the Creator would begin the fourth commandment unlike any of the other nine, with the imperative word *remember* attached to the gift day He had bequeathed to His Earth children.

And what is more, *remember* is an intriguing word looking in two directions. " 'Remember' can have either a retrospective (looking back) or prospective (looking forward) focus, but most often includes both functions. An example of a retrospective 'remember' might be, 'Remember the directions to my place I gave you last week, so that you don't get lost.' An example of a prospective 'remember' might be, 'Remember the directions I am about to give you to my place, so that you don't get lost trying to get here.' In either case 'remember' conveys something important that you do not want someone to forget."[20]

So that we would not forget, He carved it in granite. "Remember the Sabbath day by keeping it holy" (Exodus 20:8). And then He came to Earth to show us how.

What does all this have to do with blue laws? I repeat—I am against Sunday blue laws to solve our need for law and order because, on the authority of God's holy law, Jesus is Lord of the seventh-day Sabbath. And any attempt to legislate the religious practice of worship is doomed from the outset.

Then how in the world did we get into this confusing mess? The

Apocalypse's twin book, Daniel, reveals the story in troubling detail.

Enter now the antichrist. A long line of Protestant reformers, including Martin Luther and John Knox, poured over the apocalyptic books of Daniel and Revelation and identified the Dark Ages and Middle Ages church in Rome as the predicted coming antichrist.[21] One of the critical prophetic pieces of evidence that led them to their conclusion was one line in Daniel 7.

In vision, Daniel has just been shown four world kingdoms—Babylon, Media-Persia, Greece, and Rome. And when the fourth kingdom appears before him as a dreadful iron-fanged beast, clawing its way out of a wind-swept sea, its head spiked with ten horns, Daniel is stunned: "While I was thinking about the horns, there before me was another horn, a little one, which came up among them; and three of the first horns were uprooted before it. This horn had eyes like the eyes of a human being and a mouth that spoke boastfully" (Daniel 7:8).

A terrible beast, a pompous horn speaking boastfully (the Apocalypse depicts this same sea beast speaking "blasphemies"[22]) against God (i.e., it is anti-God) and ruthlessly persecuting the holy people of God. Who or what is this terror?

"He will speak against the Most High and oppress his holy people and try to change the set times and the laws. The holy people will be delivered into his hands for a time, times and half a time" (Daniel 7:25).

Here again is that apocalyptic time packet of 1,260 days symbolizing 1,260 years.[23] This little-horn power that springs up out of the old Roman Empire (Daniel's fourth beast kingdom) would rule during the dark and bloody Middle Ages. English political philosopher Thomas Hobbes (1588–1679), in his lengthy 1651 treatise *Leviathan* identified that power (quoted here in Old English spelling and grammar): "And if a man consider the originall of this great Ecclesiasticall Dominion, he will easily perceive, that the *Papacy*, is no other, than the *Ghost* of the deceased *Romane Empire*, sitting crowned upon the grave thereof: For so did the Papacy start up on a Sudden out of the Ruines of that Heathen Power."[24]

The antichrist would be both a religious and political power. Hobbes, Luther, the Reformers all unabashedly identified this apocalyptic geo-religio-political power as the papacy. And what did Daniel predict this power would do? "He will speak against the Most High and oppress his holy people and try to change the set times and the laws" (Daniel 7:25). The little-horn antichrist power would set about to change God's holy times and God's holy laws in its defiance of the Most High God.

And what did Rome claim to have changed? Both the Ten

Commandments and the seventh-day Sabbath. Can we prove that? Here, in its own words, are Rome's boastful claims.

In *The Convert's Catechism*, an instructional book for those who join the Roman Catholic Church, is this teaching:

> Question: Which is the Sabbath day?
> Answer: Saturday is the Sabbath day.
> Question: Why do we observe Sunday instead of Saturday?
> Answer: We observe Sunday instead of Saturday because the Catholic Church transferred the solemnity from Saturday to Sunday.[25]

"He will . . . try to change the set times and the laws" (Daniel 7:25).

Cardinal James Gibbons, in his popular *Faith of Our Fathers* (by 1980 in its 111th printing), is just as clear: "You may read the Bible from Genesis to Revelation and you will not find a single line authorizing the sanctification of Sunday. The Scriptures enforce the religious observance of Saturday."[26]

Then why does Rome venerate Sunday? *The Catholic Encyclopedia* answers that question like so: "The Church . . . after changing the day of rest from the Jewish Sabbath, or seventh day of the week, to the first, made the Third Commandment refer to Sunday as the day to be kept holy as the Lord's Day."[27]

Third Commandment? Everyone knows the Sabbath commandment, as recorded in the Bible, is the fourth commandment. Why the discrepancy? Because long ago Rome in her catechisms (small books for teaching new believers Roman Catholic faith) removed the second commandment from the Ten Commandments—"You shall not make for yourself an image . . ." (Exodus 20:4)—in order to accommodate her popular use of images in prayer, liturgy, and architecture. To make up for the missing commandment, Rome, in her catechisms, then divided the Tenth Commandment into two commandments, thus maintaining a necessary total of ten. But that the ten commandments of Rome's catechism are not God's Ten Commandments of Holy Scripture is disturbingly apparent.

"He will . . . try to change the set times and the laws" (Daniel 7:25). Daniel predicted this dark Middle Ages power would do just that—change God's holy day and revise God's holy law.

But if the Catholic Church claims to have changed the Sabbath from Saturday to Sunday, why do most Protestant churches also worship on Sunday? A good question, and one that Catholics themselves also ask.

In his book, *The Faith of Millions*, the late John A. O'Brien, priest and former professor at University of Notre Dame, wrote:

> But since Saturday, not Sunday, is specified in the Bible, isn't it curious that non-Catholics who profess to take their religion directly from the Bible and not from the Church, observe Sunday instead of Saturday? Yes, of course, it is inconsistent; but this change was made about fifteen centuries before Protestantism was born, and by that time the custom was universally observed. *They have continued the custom, even though it rests upon the authority of the Catholic Church and not upon an explicit text in the Bible.* That observance remains as a reminder of the Mother Church from which the non-Catholic sects [Protestants] broke away—like a boy running away from home but still carrying in his pocket a picture of his mother or a lock of her hair.[28]

Say what you will about that simile of a runaway boy carrying his mother's picture in his pocket, O'Brien is certainly forthright in his assertion that Protestants who worship on Sunday, not having a single Bible text to stand on, are left with the only plausible explanation for their first-day veneration of Sunday as God's Sabbath: *they are imitating the example of Rome.* They have no other excuse.

"He will . . . try to change the set times and the laws" (Daniel 7:25).

And that is why I am against Sunday blue laws as a law-and-order solution. Because I fear blue laws one day will attempt to legislate the wrong day (the first day) in place of the right day (the seventh day). The fact that the antichrist power has already legislated that unbiblical substitution centuries ago only increases the odds the American government one day will do the same. (In just a few pages, you are about to see an America you never dreamed possible. Whatever you do, do not skip the next chapter.)

In the meantime, suffice it to say it is no wonder God's last "law and order" appeal to the human race is an urgent call to worship Him as Creator on His seventh-day Sabbath. Just before the Apocalypse depicts the second coming of Jesus (Revelation 14:14), it details God's final appeal to humanity: "Then I saw another angel flying in midair, and he had the eternal gospel to proclaim to those who live on the earth—to every nation, tribe, language and people. He said in a loud voice [in Greek, *magale phone*, which in English translates to "megaphone"], 'Fear God and give him glory, because the hour of his judgment has come. *Worship him who made the heavens, the earth, the sea and the springs of water* " (Revelation 14:6, 7; emphasis added).

If the last line of this urgent universal appeal sounds familiar, it is because it comes from the last verse of the fourth commandment: "For in six days *the* Lord *made the heavens and the earth, the sea, and all that is in them,* but he rested on the seventh day. Therefore the Lord blessed the Sabbath day and made it holy" (Exodus 20:11; emphasis added).

In other words, what immediately precedes the second coming of Jesus is God's last passionate megaphone cry to the human race: "Wake up, world—it's judgment time! Come back to your Creator and worship Him *now* on His seventh-day Sabbath—we are running out of time!"

Not surprisingly, the final issue on this planet will be a question of authority. *Who has the authority to command my allegiance?* Christ my Creator, who died for me—or an antichrist power that could care less for me? Which day I worship on reveals which authority I depend upon.

Who has the authority to command my obedience? When they were arrested, Peter and the apostles were unequivocal: "We must obey God rather than human beings" (Acts 5:29). The coming Sunday blue laws on steroids cannot change the appeal and must not change our response.

The Bible declares, "Choose for yourselves this day whom you will serve. . . . As for me and my household, we will serve the Lord" (Joshua 24:15).

Or in the words of Martin Luther, the spiritual father of Protestantism: "Here I stand. I can do no other. God help me! Amen."[29]

---

1. Wikipedia, s.v. "Blue Law," last modified May 8, 2021, https://en.wikipedia.org/wiki/Blue_law.

2. Wikipedia, s.v. "Blue Law."

3. George McCready Price, *Time of the End* (Nashville, TN: Southern Publishing Association, 1967), 111.

4. Price.

5. Abraham Heschel, *The Sabbath*, paperback ed. (New York: Farrar, Straus and Giroux, 2005), 21.

6. Sigve Tonstad, *The Lost Meaning of the Seventh Day* (Berrien Springs, MI: Andrews University Press, 2009), 96.

7. "I appeared to Abraham, to Isaac and to Jacob as God Almighty, but by my name the Lord I did not make myself fully known to them" (Exodus 6:3).

8. "When the Lord finished speaking to Moses on Mount Sinai, he gave him the two tablets of the covenant law, the tablets of stone inscribed by the finger of God" (Exodus 31:18).

9. Tonstad, *Lost Meaning*, 96.

10. Tonstad, 108.

11. See John 1:1–3; Colossians 1:16, 17; Hebrews 1:2.

12. Heschel, *Sabbath*, 21.

13. Skip MacCarty, "The Seventh-Day Sabbath," in *Perspectives on the Sabbath: Four Views*, ed. Christopher Donato (Nashville, TN: B&H Academic, 2011), 21.

14. J. H. Gerstner, "Law in the NT," in *ISBE*, ed. G. W. Bromiley (Grand Rapids, MI: Eerdmans, 1986), 3:85, quoted in MacCarty, "*The Seventh-Day Sabbath*," 21.

15. Skip MacCarty, *Sabbath: 'Was Made For Man'* (Berrien Springs, MI: Andrews University Press, forthcoming), emphasis added.

16. Jacques Doukhan, *Secrets of Revelation: The Apocalypse Through Hebrew Eyes* (Hagerstown, MD: Review and Herald, 2002), 21.

17. Doukhan.

18. Doukhan adds a further dimension to the concept of the Lord's Day: "It is likewise highly probable that Yohanan is alluding to the other 'Day of the Lord,' the *Yom YHWH* of the ancient Hebrew prophets (Isa. 13:9–13; Eze. 30:1–5; Joel 2:1–11; Amos 5:18–20; Zeph. 1:14–18; etc), the day of judgment and the day of His coming at the end of times. The eschatological context of our passage confirms such an interpretation. In other words, Yohanan received his vision about the day of the Lord (day of final judgment and of the *Parousia*) during the Sabbath day (the other day of the Lord). That the prophet has associated the two days is not unusual. The Sabbath has always had eschatological overtones in the Bible (Isa. 58:14; 61:1–3), as well as in Jewish tradition, which understands the Sabbath as the sign of the day of deliverance and 'the foretaste of the World-to-come.' " Doukhan, 21, 22.

19. MacCarty, "*The Seventh-Day Sabbath*," 35, 37.

20. Skip MacCarty, *The Set-apart Commandment* (Berrien Springs, MI: Andrews University Press, forthcoming).

21. In his book, *On the Babylonian Captivity of the Church*, Martin Luther wrote: "If they [the pope and all the Romanists] do not abrogate all their laws and traditions, restore proper liberty to the churches of Christ, and cause that liberty to be taught, then they are guilty of all the souls that perish in this miserable servitude, and that the papacy is identical with the kingdom of Babylon and the Antichrist itself." Quoted in James M. Kittelson, *Luther the Reformer: The Story of the Man and His Career* (Minneapolis, MN: Fortress Press, 2003), 152.

22. See Revelation 13:5.

23. Note that 3½ prophetic years equals 1,260 days in prophecy, which equals 1,260 years in history (see pp. 47, 48 for details).

24. Thomas Hobbes, *Leviathan* (Cambridge, UK: Cambridge University Press, 1904), 516, https://www.google.com/books/edition/Leviathan/2oc6AAAAMAAJ?hl=en&gbpv=1&bsq=papacy; emphasis in original.

25. Peter Geiermann, *Converts Catechism of Catholic Doctrine* (St. Louis, MO: B. Herder, 1910), 50, http://handle.slv.vic.gov.au/10381/189334.

26. James Gibbons, *Faith of Our Fathers*, 50th ed. (Baltimore: John Murphy and Co., 1898), 111, 112, https://www.google.com/books/edition/The_Faith_of_Our_Fathers/Yfygm8HHdbsC?hl=en&gbpv=1&printsec=frontcover.

27. Charles G. Herbermann, ed., et al., *The Catholic Encyclopedia*, vol. 4, s.v. "Commandments of God" (New York: Robert Appleton Company, 1908), 153, https://books.google.com/books?id=MIY_AQAAMAAJ&printsec=frontcoverno. v=onepage&q&f=false.

28. John A. O'Brien, *The Faith of Millions: The Credentials of the Catholic Religion*, rev. 4th ed.n (Huntington, IN: Our Sunday Visitor Publishing, 1974), 400, 401; emphasis added.

29. Martin Luther, quoted in Kittelson, *Luther the Reformer*, 161.

When we are faced with a disaster,

whether as individuals, a community,

or even a nation, the sudden cataclysm

shakes loose what once were deeply

rooted values and beliefs.

IS THE RELIGIOUS RIGHT WRONG?

Did you hear what NASA pulled off? They tore a page out of science fiction and actually landed a spacecraft on an asteroid. No kidding! Their target asteroid (named Bennu) is about as tall as the Empire State Building and is spinning while it orbits 200 million miles away from us. So the scientists at NASA not only rocketed this small craft the 200 million miles to Bennu—they landed it on the asteroid, grabbed a sample of grit from that rocky surface, re-thrusted the engines, and began flying the spacecraft back to Earth, with a projected ETA of September 24, 2023, in the barren Utah desert![1] God bless America.

But here's the question: What if there were an asteroid out there—unidentified, currently unseen—that comes out of nowhere and slams into this planetary home of ours? (We noted that foreboding possibility here in a previous chapter, "Calamities Most Awful, Most Unexpected.")

I received an email from a geologist friend of mine who happened to watch a presentation I made on asteroids. She wrote:

> Your sermon this a.m. WOKE ME UP. So an asteroid hits SF [San Francisco] or LA [Los Angeles]. Millions die, but why would other countries tremble in fear? [She is referring to Jesus' warning in Luke 21:26—"People will faint from terror, apprehensive of what is coming on the world, for the heavenly bodies will be shaken."] Because [and now she answers her own question] if the asteroid triggers a Richter scale 10 on the San Andreas Fault, I have been told the Earth will ring like a bell. I think the chains of fault systems around the world would be activated. The destruction of all the major cities and some nuclear plants sitting on faults will get everyone's attention. The ground will tremble world-wide. The tsunamis will make our oceans roar [again quoting Jesus in Luke 21:25]. Add to all of this the activation of the

volcanic chaos, and yes, globally, people will tremble in fear. [All from] one asteroid.[2]

And how many asteroids—30 meters and larger—does NASA estimate there are in our solar system? Two million, with only eighteen thousand of them spotted and identified so far. So say an unidentified one gets through and strikes this planet.

A social scientist at the University of New York at Buffalo, Michael Barkun, researched the effect disasters can have on people's attitudes and published his fascinating but troubling findings in his book, *Disasters and the Millennium*. In reporting on those findings, Marvin Moore, in his own provocative book, *Could It Really Happen?*, writes, "One of [Barkun's] most significant conclusions was that 'disaster creates conditions peculiarly fitted to *the rapid alteration of belief systems.*' "[3]

Given what we are about to discover in the Apocalypse, hold on to that line: " 'The rapid alteration of belief systems.' " And how do disasters contribute to this " 'rapid alteration' "? Barkun's research concluded: " 'Disaster produces the questioning, the anxiety, and the suggestibility that are required [for change]; only in its wake are people moved to abandon values of the past.' "[4] That is, when we are faced with a disaster, whether as individuals, a community, or even a nation, the sudden cataclysm shakes loose what once were deeply rooted values and beliefs.

" 'Belief systems which under nondisaster conditions might be dismissed, now receive sympathetic consideration.' "

" 'A disaster population suffers a temporary sense of incapacity, vulnerability, and confusion. The collapsed social structure renders traditional authority relationships less effective and traditional statuses less meaningful.' " And what is the result? " 'Belief systems which under nondisaster conditions might be dismissed, now receive sympathetic consideration.' "[5]

That is, what you earlier would have rejected out of hand—a contrary idea, an unacceptable notion, or a previously rejected suggestion—now suddenly, because of the catastrophe and the ensuing confusion, your mind is opened to accept what you previously found implausible. What we would have categorically rejected before the disaster, we now embrace. Or vice versa what we previously embraced, we now reject. It cuts both ways.

And by the way, it doesn't have to be an asteroid strike. It could be a killer earthquake, an imploding political upheaval, a government coup, a debilitating economic collapse, a civil war—all of which rank as disasters for sure.

Enter now Revelation 13 and the mark of the beast—a stunning, predicted scenario that will become a tragic reality literally overnight in the face of what has to be some unnamed cataclysmic disaster. How else can we describe such a mass global repudiation of values once considered timeless? For a moment, let's review the key players on this apocalyptic stage.

> Then I saw a second beast, coming out of the earth. It had two horns like a lamb, but it spoke like a dragon (Revelation 13:11).

Remember the earth beast? Indeed, we do. But say, "Earth beast," and the phrase immediately conjures up a picture of the sea beast, the raging opening act to this thirteenth (and tragically unlucky) chapter of the Apocalypse. Because the curtain rises in Revelation 13 to a nondescript amalgamation of a part-leopard, part-bear, part-lion beastly nightmare with seven bellowing heads sporting ten horns, each bedecked with a crown (Greek *diadema*, or "diadem") of rulership. There she roars, dripping the brine of the sea from which she has emerged, this freakish creature, as freakish as the seven-headed dragon who is her creator. No wonder, then, the names of blasphemy posted on each of her gyrating heads and necks—she is, after all, like her red dragon creator, a pseudo-religious power, raging her way through global deception into global dominance. If you don't believe it, just read her vita for yourself:

> The dragon gave the [sea] beast his power and his throne and great authority. One of the heads of the beast seemed to have had a fatal wound, but the fatal wound had been healed. The whole world was filled with wonder and followed the beast. People worshiped the dragon because he had given authority to the beast, and they also worshiped the beast and asked, "Who is like the beast? Who can wage war against it?" (Revelation 13:2–4).

The sea beast not only sports names of blasphemy upon her heads but she also, with nary a word of protest, gladly receives the fawning worship of a fallen world. No secular power or atheistic institution would covet religious worship. But the sea beast does. After all, she does not wear her seven diadems for nothing. With naked ambition, she will rule the world, "the whole world," as the Apocalypse is quick to warn in Revelation 13:3.

The apocalyptic prophecies of Daniel 7 and Revelation 13, uncannily univocal in their warning of this dread power, were the prophetic basis for the Protestant Reformers' identification of the sea beast as the antichrist power that ruthlessly ruled the nations from Rome during the dark and bloody Middle Ages.

But the papacy was mortally wounded.

> One of the heads of the beast seemed to have had a fatal wound. . . .
>
> "If anyone is to go into captivity,
>   into captivity they will go.
> If anyone is to be killed with the sword,
>   with the sword they will be killed."
>
> This calls for patient endurance and faithfulness on the part of God's people (Revelation 13:3, 10).

She, who had slaughtered the saints by the tens of thousands (some estimate millions), received her own mortal wounding and was taken into captivity, as the Apocalypse predicted. "The tremendous storm of the French Revolution was about to break and to sweep away the church, with the nobility, the throne, and kindred ancient institutions. The Revolutionary leaders were filled with the rationalistic spirit. . . . In 1798 Rome was made a republic by French arms, and Pope Pius VI (1775–1799) carried a prisoner to France, where he died."[6] Wounded!

But at the very time of the sea beast's wounding, it is no coincidence that the earth beast springs into international recognition and prominence in the late 1700s (just as the Apocalypse indicated).

> Then [after the sea beast's wounding] I saw a second beast, coming out of the earth. It had two horns like a lamb, but it spoke like a dragon (Revelation 13:11).

Growing like a weed out of the barren earth of the New World, the earth beast (as the second half of Revelation 13 dramatically corroborates) eventually achieves global superpower status. And the rest is history, the celebrated but eventually tragic history of the United States of America.

"For decades, the U.S. has enjoyed global military dominance, an achievement that has underpinned its influence, national security and efforts at promoting democracy. The Department of Defense spends more than $700 billion a year on weaponry and combat preparedness—more than the next 10 countries combined [including Russia, China, Germany, France, the United Kingdom, and Japan], according to [the] economic think tank the Peter G. Peterson Foundation. The U.S. military's reach is vast and empire-like."[7]

How else can you explain the global dominance this confederacy between the sea beast and the earth beast will inflict upon the world, as foretold in Revelation 13? "Empire-like" indeed.

But the earth beast's beginnings seemed to be such a narrative of innocence and even Christlikeness, as the "two horns like a lamb" described in verse 11 would suggest. After all, here was a land that championed the twin values of civil liberty and religious liberty.

Take Roger Williams, the fugitive Baptist minister who founded Rhode Island in the early 1600s and America's first champion of religious liberty:

> [Roger] Williams established the first area [colony] to practice the separation of church and state in the New World. To merge the two, he held, harmed not only democracy but religion as well. . . . Williams believed the only "true" religions were based on a voluntary and free conscience. . . . He codified the idea that the government could rule only in civil matters. As such, the Providence government could not punish those who violated the religious principles contained in the Ten Commandments, such as "idolatry, Sabbathbreaking, false worship, and blasphemy. . . . The laws of the First Table of the Ten Commandments [Williams taught] are not regulations for civil society or a political order. They belong to the realm of religion, not politics."[8]

And so, for two and half centuries, America has championed the separation of church and state—and rightfully so—favoring neither religion over government nor government over religion, as Roger Williams taught us.

But something dreadful happens. This global superpower begins to speak "like a dragon"! Talk about a forked tongue! What a sad reversal for this one-time champion of liberty and freedom. "Revelation 13 shows that the United States of America, which in the post-medieval period provided protection and a safe haven to the church, will play *the key role in last day events.*"[9] How sad, how utterly sad.

Enter now, earth beast phase 2:

> Then I saw a second beast, coming out of the earth. It had two horns like a lamb, but it spoke like a dragon. It [the earth beast] exercised all the authority of the first beast [the sea beast] on its behalf, and made the earth and its inhabitants worship the first beast, whose fatal wound had been healed (Revelation 13:11, 12).

How could that even be humanly, conceivably possible—in a freedom-loving, church-and-state-separating land like America? It is indeed inconceivable, *until* or *unless* some sort of cataclysmic disaster is factored into the equation. It is clear something has gone terribly wrong—to the place where not only the citizens of the United States but also the inhabitants of the entire planet are so shaken and threatened

But something dreadful happens. This global superpower begins to speak "like a dragon"!

that, in a state of cognitive confusion, they allow the abrogation of the very freedoms and liberties they once so ardently championed. They allow a secular government, confederated with a religious power, to force them to an act of spiritual worship.

Something horrible has transpired. And we are not told what. Oh yes, we have been given ample evidence of conditions on the earth when time runs out for our human civilization. Daniel described the end of the world this way: "There will be a time of distress such as has not happened from the beginning of nations until then" (Daniel 12:1). Jesus Himself depicted Earth's final chapter:

> For then there will be great distress, unequaled from the beginning of the world until now—and never to be equaled again.
>
> If those days had not been cut short, no one would survive, but for the sake of the elect those days will be shortened (Matthew 24:21, 22).

Whatever calamity or disaster has transpired in Revelation 13, it threatens the existence of the entire planet, including God's people!

What was it that Michael Barkun's research discovered? " 'Disaster produces the questioning, the anxiety, and the suggestibility that are required [for change]; only in its wake are people moved to abandon values of the past.' "[10]

What old values of the past will America abandon? Keep reading.

> Then I saw a second beast, coming out of the earth. It had two horns like a lamb, but it spoke like a dragon. It exercised all the authority of the first beast on its behalf, and made the earth and its inhabitants worship the first beast, whose fatal wound had been healed. And it performed great signs, even causing fire to come down from heaven to the earth in full view of the people (Revelation 13:11–13).

Sounds like the Mount Carmel showdown, does it not? A showdown of the gods over worship, no less! Except the dragon will pull off a reversed form of Mount Carmel. Rather than a scenario like Elijah turning people *back* to the Creator God, this superpower confederacy does the opposite. Imitating the priests of Baal, it turns the world *away* from the Creator. Which, no surprise, has been the ambition of the dragon from the beginning— the dragon who is, of course, the most anti-Christ of all.

"The beast bringing fire down from heaven also counterfeits the day of Pentecost, when tongues of fire came down from heaven upon the disciples (Acts 2:3). All of this shows that bringing fire down from heaven is designed to counterfeit the power of God to deceive people and persuade them that these miraculous signs are the manifestations of divine power."[11]

Should we, who live in a visually dominated culture where seeing is believing, be surprised with this display of physical "virtual reality" signs crafted to deceive the whole earth? Hardly. "The coming of the lawless one will be in accordance with how Satan works. He will use all sorts of displays [i.e., visual evidences] of power through signs and wonders that serve the lie" (2 Thessalonians 2:8, 9). And look for America to be the dragon's endgame playground.

> Because of the signs it was given power to perform on behalf of the first beast, it [the earth beast] deceived the inhabitants of the

earth. It ordered them to set up an image in honor of the beast who was wounded by the sword and yet lived [the sea beast]. The second beast was given power to give breath to the image of the first beast, so that the image could speak and cause all who refused to worship the image to be killed (Revelation 13:14, 15).

Why, this is the story of Shadrach, Meshach, and Abednego in spades. Everybody knows the dramatic narrative of those three young Hebrew men who refused to bow down and worship the king of Babylon's image of gold. Oh yes, they understood the egomaniacal king's explicit command. But to borrow from the Apocalypse for this drama in Daniel, "They did not love their lives so much as to shrink from death" (Revelation 12:11). Their sentence? A fiery furnace, already red-hot but stoked seven times hotter!

It's hard to believe it, let alone picture it! The day is coming when this earth beast–sea beast superpower confederacy creates an image to the antichrist beast and then, wielding the threat of capital punishment—that is right, the sentence of death—for those who resist, commands the entire world to bow down and worship it. Hard to believe. Although with the erosion of this nation's cherished values in this hour of America's waning, it is not as hard to believe as it once was, is it?

It [the earth beast] also forced all people, great and small, rich and poor, free and slave, to receive a mark on their right hands or on their foreheads, so that they could not buy or sell unless they had the mark, which is the name of the beast or the number of its name (Revelation 13:16, 17).

There it is—the dreaded and mysterious mark of the beast. But no matter how hard we protest this radical U-turn of values, the question still begs itself: How in the name of freedom-loving, church-and-state-separating America could this possibly be?

Richard Evans, in his book *The Coming of the Third Reich*, presciently asks four probing questions about Germany that are pertinent to our own nation today: "How was it that an advanced and highly cultured nation such as Germany could give in to the brutal force of National Socialism so quickly and so easily? Why was there such little serious resistance to the Nazi takeover? How could an insignificant party of the radical right rise to power with dramatic suddenness? Why did so many Germans fail to perceive the potentially disastrous consequences of ignoring the violent, racist and murderous nature of the Nazi movement?"[12]

Permit me to add four additional similar questions. How could a man like Adolf Hitler walk away with the churches of Germany in his hip pocket? Where was the Christian resistance to a ruler and party so anti-Christ in their governance? And when Hitler rallied the nation to blame the Jews for Germany's collective ills, why did so preciously few religious leaders challenge his corrupted logic regarding that community of Sabbatarians? Instead, the clergy of that nation were currying a place at the Führer's table while he was planning his endgame for the eradication of the nation's Jewish minority. I always have been and will be suspicious of men and women who are professionally (as well as personally) ostensibly devoted to the mission of Christ and the church yet jockey for political recognition or a presidential invitation to the table of power. Thirty pieces of silver is the price for lusting after political prominence and power.

This leads me to one more question: Is it happening all over again in America? I received an email from one of our viewers: "I see you're going to talk about the religious right—don't forget the irreligious left." Fair point, and I agree. But the history of Germany is a stunning reminder that even good-hearted *Christian* men and women can be duped into embracing an antichrist set of values, all for the sake of advancing their own personal and political agendas!

How serious is this mark of the beast deception? Listen in for a moment to the third angel of Revelation 14, who, along with the first and second angel, encapsulates the Creator's final appeal to this endgame civilization:

> A third angel followed them and said in a loud voice: "If anyone worships the beast and its image and receives its mark on their forehead or on their hand, they, too, will drink the wine of God's fury, which has been poured full strength into the cup of his wrath. They will be tormented with burning sulfur in the presence of the holy angels and of the Lamb. And the smoke of their torment will rise for ever and ever. There will be no rest day or night for those who worship the beast and its image, or for anyone who receives the mark of its name" (Revelation 14:9–11).

The apocalyptic classic *The Great Controversy* describes these words of the third angel as "the most fearful threatening ever addressed to mortals."[13] Why language so strong? Given what is hugely at stake, apparently the Creator God of relentless love is left no recourse but to try to awaken

His Earth children with a final, dire warning.

We need to understand that the Apocalypse draws a dramatic contrast between what it describes as "the seal of God" and "the mark of the beast." Here is a critical identifier: *both of these markers are utterly focused on worship*. For the sake of comparison, first notice the description of the "seal of God":

> After this I saw four angels standing at the four corners of the earth, holding back the four winds of the earth to prevent any wind from blowing on the land or on the sea or on any tree. Then I saw another angel coming up from the east, having the seal of the living God. He called out in a loud voice to the four angels who had been given power to harm the land and the sea: "Do not harm the land or the sea or the trees until we put a seal on the foreheads of the servants of our God" (Revelation 7:1–3).

As Sigve Tonstad observes: "The competing marks have a representative function. For both symbols, whether the 'seal' or the 'mark,' they represent the *name* of the reality to which they point. This warrants the view that the sealing (and the marking) 'symbolizes the central dilemma of the Apocalypse.' "[14] But we need not overcomplicate these two symbols. In fact, what we have already gleaned from our cursory reading about the mark of the beast, we now know about the seal of God.

The seal of God is received only on the forehead, whereas the mark of the beast is received on the forehead or the right hand. Why the difference? Because the forehead represents the place of cognitive decision, the human power of choice that rules our lives. Thus only the mark of the beast can be applied to the hand, an apt symbolization of avoiding a difficult decision and showing a willingness to be led along, following the crowd, so to speak. Obviously, God drags no crowd into His kingdom. When it comes to a saving friendship with the Eternal, it is exclusively a matter of forehead, or personal choice, rather than by hand, or unthinking compliance. You *choose*—you must carefully, prayerfully *choose*—whom you will obey, whom you will worship. We all make that *choice*. And to not make it is to make it.

In the words of David Foster Wallace:

> In the day-to-day trenches of adult life, there is actually no such thing as atheism. There is no such thing as not worshipping.

Everybody worships. The only choice we get is what to worship. . . . If you worship money and things—if they are where you tap real meaning in life—then you will never have enough. Never feel you have enough. It's the truth. Worship your own body and beauty and sexual allure and you will always feel ugly, and when time and age start showing, you will die a million deaths before they finally plant you. . . . Worship power—you will feel weak and afraid, and you will need ever more power over others to keep the fear at bay. Worship your intellect, being seen as smart—you will end up feeling stupid, a fraud, always on the verge of being found out.[15]

He is right, is he not? We are creatures shaped by our Creator to worship. As Wallace expressed it: "There is no such thing as not worshipping." Thus the endgame on this planet comes down to a solitary choice: *What or whom shall I worship?*

For it is both compelling and clear that the seal and the mark will represent two sources of authority for humans. The mark of the beast symbolizes the authority of the antichrist (human authority). The seal of God symbolizes the authority of the Creator God (divine authority). These are the only two loci of authority in the universe—the authority of the Creator or the authority of the creature. Every human being must decide, as David Foster Wallace concluded, whom to worship, which authority will be supreme in his or her life. Plain and simple.

Jiri Moskala, dean of the Seventh-day Adventist Theological Seminary on the campus of Andrews University where I pastor, observes: "The [three angels'] message is God's response to the demands of the satanic trinity—the dragon and the sea and [earth] beasts of Revelation 13—that demands universal obedience. . . . But the three angels' message shows the holy Trinity exposing these end-time deceptions and fake news, helping people to make right choices and worship the Lord in truth."[16]

Moskala points out that between the satanic trinity and the Holy Trinity, the word *worship* appears eight times in chapters 13 and 14 of the Apocalypse. Incontrovertibly, worship is of eternal significance for humanity in the endgame: you will either worship and obey the Creator, or you will worship and obey the antichrist. There is no third choice or middle ground. In the final stage of the cosmic battle on Earth between Christ and Satan—between the Lamb and the dragon—it will come down to these two choices:

1. "Worship Him who made the heavens, the earth, the sea and the springs of waters" (Revelation 14:7).

   Or:

2. "The [earth] beast [America] was given power to give breath to the image of the [sea] beast [Rome], so that the image could speak and cause all who refused to worship the image to be killed" (Revelation 13:15).

The truth is the Creator could not be clearer. Here is the fourth commandment of His Ten Commandments: "Remember the Sabbath day by keeping it holy. . . . For in six days the LORD made the heavens and the earth, the sea, and all that is in them, but he rested the seventh day. Therefore the LORD blessed the Sabbath day and made it holy" (Exodus 20:8–11).

A few Christmases ago, my wife, Karen, gave me a nifty chrome device whereby I can stamp my initials and the words *Library of Dwight K. Nelson* in any book I have in my library. It's called a seal. And if I were president of the United States (you can be thankful I am not and be assured I never will be), I would have my own seal to prove my authority for any executive order I signed. The seal would read thus:

- My name—Dwight K. Nelson
- My office—president
- My jurisdiction—United States of America

When the president of the United States of America affixes the seal of that office on a law, that seal proves the authenticity of the president's authority.

Did you know that God has a seal with His name, His office, and His jurisdiction clearly indicated in it? We just read it in the fourth commandment of the Ten Commandments: "Remember the Sabbath day by keeping it holy. . . . For in six days the LORD [His name] made [His office, Creator] the heavens and the earth, the sea, and all that is in them [His jurisdiction], but he rested the seventh day. Therefore the LORD blessed the Sabbath day and made it holy" (Exodus 20:8–11). God has His very unique, exclusive personal seal:

- His name—the Lord
- His office—Creator
- His jurisdiction—the universe

The seventh-day Sabbath is God's seal of authority as the Creator of the universe. And when I worship Him on His Day, I declare my allegiance to His authority alone. As Tonstad notes: "To receive the seal of the living God ([Revelation] 7:2) is best understood as an inward matter. 'In its deepest sense this sealing means the outward manifestation of character. The hidden goodness of God's servants is at last blazoned outwardly, and the divine name that was written in secret by God's Spirit on their hearts [Ephesians 1:13–14; 4:30] is now engraved openly on their brows by the very signet ring [seal] of the living God.' "[17]

In contradistinction and opposition to the seal of God, "the mark of the beast" is a counter-authority seal. Could the Roman Catholic Church be clearer? "Sunday is *our mark of authority.* . . . The Church is above the Bible, and this transference of Sabbath observance is proof of that fact."[18] There they both are—again, plain and simple—the seal of God in His seventh-day Sabbath and the mark of the beast in Sunday, Rome's substitute day of worship.

Incontrovertibly, worship is of eternal significance for humanity in the endgame: you will either worship and obey the Creator, or you will worship and obey the antichrist. There is no third choice or middle ground.

And in the end, the majority—"the whole world" (Revelation 13:3)—will accept the command of this superpower confederacy and will receive its mark. In contrast, a small minority will refuse to comply with the worship of the image and will not receive the mark. The Apocalypse describes this minority—

Here is the patience of the saints; here are those who keep the commandments of God and the faith of Jesus (Revelation 14:12, NKJV).

The dragon was enraged with the woman, and he went to make war with the rest of her offspring, who keep the commandments of God and have the testimony of Jesus Christ (Revelation 12:17).

Thus once again, it really does come down to a simple choice: Whose authority takes precedence in your life—God's or man's? Whom will we worship and obey—Christ the Creator or the dragon and his antichrist? The results are stark. Worship the Creator and receive the seal of God. Worship the antichrist and receive the mark of the beast. And by that marker, the last generation on Earth will decide its destiny.

Does anybody have the mark of the beast today? Not one person, simply because the sea beast and the earth beast have yet to consolidate their superpower confederacy. But the fracturing polarizations shaping into reality across this land (and around the globe)—evidenced now in politics, culture, race, finances, and the existential soul of what it means to be an American today—all point to this accelerating showdown between the divine Trinity and the demonic trinity. We are all players (in some cases, pawns) in the endgame.

In the meantime, there are thousands of Christians, along with their pastors, who worship Jesus on Sunday, sincerely but mistakenly believing it is the Lord's Day. Their belief, of course, does not make Sunday God's sacred Sabbath. But should they discover—as they most certainly will one day—the day they worship on has never been sanctioned by their Creator, which way do you suppose the friends of Jesus will choose?

As I mentioned earlier, growing up in Japan, I used to ride the trains to school every day. When Karen and I went back to Tokyo a few years ago, we got on a train, sat down, and were thoroughly enjoying the ride. But then I happened to look up at the railway map posted on the inside of the train. I studied it long and hard and finally came to the disconcerting realization we were headed in the wrong direction—because we were on *the wrong train*!

Let me tell you something about Japanese trains. Once you discover you have the right ticket but you are on the wrong train, you have two choices. You may stay on the wrong train and keep going to where you never wanted to go. Or you may find out which train is going the direction you want to be going and change trains. It's that simple.

Today God is calling humanity to change trains and worship Him as our Creator. The antichrist commands, "Come *this* way," but he will take you where you *never* wanted to go. The Creator invites, "Come *this* way, and I'll take you where you've *always* wanted to go."

How does Jesus put it? "Come to Me . . . ," is His invitation, "and I will give you rest" (Matthew 11:28, NKJV). "If you love Me . . . ," is His reminder, "keep My commandments" (John 14:15, NKJV). Because any way you put it, the truth is this—when it comes to the Sabbath, it has *always* been *all* about *Jesus*.

1. "NASA's OSIRIS-REx Spacecraft Successfully Touches Asteroid," OSIRIS-REx, NASA, October 20, 2020, https://www.nasa.gov/press-release/nasa-s-osiris-rex-spacecraft-successfully-touches-asteroid.

2. Elaine Kennedy, email message to author, October 10, 2020.

3. Marvin Moore, *Could It Really Happen?* (Nampa, ID: Pacific Press®, 2007), 239; emphasis added.

4. Michael Barkun, *Disaster and the Millenium*, reprint ed. (Syracuse, NY: Syracuse University Press, 1986), 6, quoted in Moore, *Could It Really Happen?*, 239.

5. Barkun, *Disaster*, 55, 56, quoted in Moore, *Could It Really Happen?*, 239.

6. Williston Walker, *A History of the Christian Church*, 3rd ed. (New York: Charles Scribner's Sons, 1970), 521.

7. Kim Hjelmgaard, " 'A Reckoning Is Near': America Has a Vast Overseas Military Empire. Does It Still Need It?," *USA TODAY*, February 25, 2021, https://www.usatoday.com/in-depth/news/world/2021/02/25/us-military-budget-what-can-global-bases-do-vs-covid-cyber-attacks/6419013002/.

8. Ron Capshaw, "Radical Roger," *Liberty*, September/October 2020, 6.

9. Ranko Stefanovic, *Plain Revelation* (Berrien Springs, MI: Andrews University Press, 2013), 160; emphasis added.

10. Barkun, *Disaster*, 6, quoted in Moore, *Could It Really Happen?*, 239.

11. Stefanovic, *Plain Revelation*, 161.

12. Richard J. Evans, *The Coming of the Third Reich* (New York: Penguin, 2003), xxii, quoted in Marvin Moore, *Could It Really Happen?*, 232.

13. Ellen G. White, *The Great Controversy* (Mountain View, CA: Pacific Press®, 1950), 449.

14. Sigve Tonstad, *Revelation* (Grand Rapids, MI: Baker Academic, 2019) 196.

15. Drake, "Everybody Worships: David Foster Wallace on Real Freedom and the Skeleton of Every Great Story," Mockingbird, September 20, 2008, https://mbird.com/2008/09/more-david-foster-wallace-quotes/.

16. Jiri Moskala, "Theological Essence: The Gospel of Revelation 14," *Adventist Review*, October 2020, 23.

17. Tonstad, *Revelation*, 132.

18. "Sabbath Observance," *Catholic Record*, September 1, 1923, quoted in Howard Peth, *7 Mysteries Solved* (Fallbrook, CA: HART Books, 2002), 749.

Is the Reformation over? We can be certain, it is safe to conclude, that there is an enemy whose dark design is to bring that mighty epoch of Christian history to a whimpering end.

A REFORMATION ON LIFE SUPPORT

It is one of those picture-perfect postcard moments. The late afternoon sun piercing through the deciduous trees that ring the plaza, on the cobbled stones a palette of red, gold, and yellow-orange leaves fallen and now scattering before the hurried but determined steps of a young man. His tonsured hair a sure sign of his life station, a monk. An agitated monk, the twitching lines of his clenched jaw a dead giveaway. In one hand, a mallet and some iron tacks. In the other, a sheath of parchments, covered in black-inked, handwritten notes. All of it now organized and collected into a single daunting challenge—ninety-five challenges to be exact. And when he strides up to the familiar town bulletin board, the creaky wooden doors of the castle church, little does the young priest know that when he nails up these ninety-five challenges to the theology and hierarchy of the reigning Middle Ages church, little does he know that with each thump of his mallet, he is unwittingly launching an ecclesiastical war that will crush the hegemony of that corrupted geo-religio-political power. Young Martin has no idea; such is the naivety of youth. He is about to become this war's leading antagonist and its dreaded lead protestor.

That picture-perfect postcard moment, which nobody knew was happening, occurred on October 31, 1517, in the German town of Wittenberg. Those ninety-five theses became the first igniting spark of an eventual religious conflagration we still remember today as the Protestant Reformation.

But is the Reformation over? As the sea beast of Revelation 13 slowly but surely regains her global hegemony, where are the protestors, the children of these ancient Protestants, to challenge this once-again burgeoning kingdom? Or is the Reformation over?

I have a book in my library that asks that very question, written by the evangelical Protestant scholar Mark Noll: *Is the Reformation Over? An Evangelical Assessment of Contemporary Roman Catholicism.*

A number of the dialogues [recent theological conversations between Roman Catholic and evangelical scholars] led to the cancellation of anathemas that had been issued during the Reformation. Even granting a certain artificiality to what the dialogues accomplished—even, that is, recognizing that goodwill may have occasionally triumphed over hardheaded realism—the cumulative results of these dialogues record a momentous shaking of once-settled ground. On the basis of the ecumenical dialogues, can it be said that the Reformation is over? Probably not. *But a once-yawning chasm has certainly narrowed.*[1]

We will return to that line: Is the Reformation over? We can be certain, it is safe to conclude, that there is an enemy whose dark design is to bring that mighty epoch of Christian history to a whimpering end. Luther himself knew and fought that enemy constantly. Unabashedly—without apology—Luther (the mighty champion of the Lord Jesus Christ and salvation by faith) railed against the devil. In fact, on one occasion—though scholars can neither verify nor deny the incident—Luther was so furious over the devil's constant harassing of his mind and conscience, he hurled his inkwell at the devil, the bottle breaking and splashing against the wall. (Tourists to the castle from 1650 until about a century ago actually saw the splatter of blue ink on the wall. But over the ensuing almost three hundred years, souvenir hunters have removed all the splattered plaster!)[2]

In what became the battle hymn of the Reformation, Martin Luther incorporated the cosmic reality of the unseen devil—the Apocalypse's red dragon, "that ancient serpent, called the devil, or Satan, who leads the whole world astray" (Revelation 12:9)—into his "A Mighty Fortress" hymn:[3]

> And though this world, with devils filled,
> Should threaten to undo us,
> We will not fear, for God has willed,
> His truth to triumph through us.[4]

The legacy of the Protestant Reformation certainly does not lie in the missing plaster on that castle wall. Our legacy is the battle Luther launched against the kingdom of darkness, the resumption of which the third-millennial children of the Reformation must prepare for immediately! So carefully watch what you are about to see.

> Then I saw three impure spirits that looked like frogs; they came out of the mouth of the dragon, out of the mouth of the beast and out of the mouth of the false prophet (Revelation 16:13).

Frogs? Come to think of it, frogs were one of the ten plagues that fell on Egypt *just before* a nation of slaves was liberated by Almighty God. So why should we be surprised when frogs appear here in the seven last plagues *just before* Satan's hostages are set free by the return of the King of kings.

But who is this false prophet depicted in the Apocalypse's sixth plague? Remember the satanic trinity of Revelation's endgame? First, there is the red dragon, which is Satan, heaven's fallen rebel angel. Second, there is the sea beast, the apocalyptic symbol for the church that ruled the dark and bloody Middle Ages and was wounded in 1798; but with the wound now healing, she is a church that will reassert her global domination just before Jesus returns. And third is the earth beast, that global superpower springing into existence in the New World in the late 1700s (at the same time Rome was wounded) and becoming a champion of religious liberty; but it eventually revokes its liberties and forces the world to worship an image of the sea beast. For this third power player, the Apocalypse adopts the moniker "false prophet" as simply another name for the earth beast, which through "the rest of Revelation [is] called the false prophet, working miracles on behalf of the sea beast (Rev. 19:20)."[5] Which, being interpreted, means this Protestant bastion of America will become a dark hold for "demonic spirits." How can that be? Keep reading:

> Then I saw three impure spirits that looked like frogs; they came out of the mouth of the dragon, out of the mouth of the beast and out of the mouth of the false prophet. They are demonic spirits that perform signs, and they go out to the kings of the whole world, to gather them for the battle on the great day of God Almighty (Revelation 16:13, 14).

It is gross to even imagine—you feel something squirming in your mouth, you open it to investigate, and out crawls or (maybe out hops a slimy, bug-eyed green frog! Imagine then the red dragon opening its mouth and out creeps this ugly green amphibian. Ditto for the sea beast. And ditto again for the earth beast. Three ugly green "demonic spirits" who materialize (certainly not as frogs) before human eyes—before the eyes of the leaders, the rulers, the kings of this planet. And when they come knocking, what do these three demonic spirits do? They "perform signs" in order to prepare world leaders and their citizens for the last great showdown battle.

Want to know who's giving the orders for these three demonic spirits to follow? "Don't let anyone deceive you in any way, for that day will not come until the rebellion occurs and the man of lawlessness is revealed, the man doomed to destruction" (2 Thessalonians 2:3).

> Mark it carefully. The name of the endgame is deception. The boots-on-the-ground strategy of the enemy in this cosmic war is *always* deception. He has always played and fought by that game plan, mixing a little truth with a whole lot of deadly error.

Mark it carefully. The name of the endgame is deception. The boots-on-the-ground strategy of the enemy in this cosmic war is *always* deception. He has always played and fought by that game plan, mixing a little truth with a whole lot of deadly error. To put it plainly, Satan is a liar! As Jesus warned the religious leaders of His day: "You belong to your father, the devil, and you want to carry out your father's desires. He was a murderer from the beginning, not holding to the truth, *for there is no truth in him.* When he lies, he speaks his native language, for he is a liar and the father of lies" (John 8:44; emphasis added). Satan is a pathological liar, and those who follow him become just like him, to the place they don't even know they are lying anymore. Mark it well, the "native language" of the satanic trinity will be lies.

"Don't let anyone deceive you in any way, for that day will not come until the rebellion occurs and the man of lawlessness is revealed, the man doomed to destruction" (2 Thessalonians 2:3). Did you catch that word, *lawlessness?* God has a law, and Satan's unsleeping effort is to destroy that law. To the extent that the dragon's endgame actually attacks the first four of God's Ten Commandments.

Ranko Stefanovic skillfully exposes this satanic attack against God's law:

Revelation shows that the first four commandments of the Decalogue—the ones that concern a person's relationship with God and worship—will become the standard of loyalty to God in the final crisis. Satan's end-time activities are portrayed in [the Apocalypse] as a well-planned attack on these four commandments:

- The sea beast's demand for worship (Rev. 13:15) is a direct attack on the first commandment: "You shall have no other gods beside Me."
- The earth beast raises up an image of the sea beast to be worshiped (13:14–15), which is a direct attack on the second commandment: "You shall not make for yourself an image. . . . You shall not worship them or serve them."
- The beast's blasphemy of God (13:5–6) is a direct attack on the third commandment: "You shall not take the name of the Lord your God in vain."
- The mark of the beast (13:16–17) is a direct attack on the fourth commandment: "Remember the Sabbath day, to keep it holy."[6]

There they are, the four commandments protecting our relationship with God that are under assault by Satan through his surrogates. If ever the descriptor *lawlessness* could be attached to anyone, the dragon is indeed most worthy. It is because the law declares the seventh-day Sabbath to be the Creator's timeless memorial of His six-day creation that Satan's tireless efforts have always been and will ever be (to the very end) to destroy that Sabbath. To Jesus' indictment—"There is no truth in him" (John 8:44)—can be added the charge in 2 Thessalonians 2:3 that he is the personification of "lawlessness."

That is why this single power, described by Paul as "the man of lawlessness" and by the Apocalypse as the sea beast, is but a front for Satan's insane ambition to eradicate the law of God from human society and culture, and thus propagate lawlessness.

Paul continues: "He [the man of lawlessness] will oppose and will exalt himself over everything that is called God or is worshiped, so that he sets himself up in God's temple, *proclaiming himself to be God*" (2 Thessalonians 2:4; emphasis added). Who can deny this was Lucifer's ambition from the beginning of his rebellion: "I will make myself like the Most

High" (Isaiah 14:14)? Who can deny this ambition has ruled the papal throne over the centuries? Pope Leo XIII, who in one encyclical called for "complete submission and obedience of will to the Church and to the Roman Pontiff, as to God Himself,"[7] also pronounced on behalf of the Roman pontiffs in a separate encyclical, "We hold upon this earth the place of God Almighty."[8]

"He will oppose and will exalt himself over everything that is called God or is worshiped, so that he sets himself up in God's temple, *proclaiming himself to be God*" (2 Thessalonians 2:4; emphasis added).

Both history and prophecy are clear. There is a "man of lawlessness" who will rule on Earth, declaring himself to be God and receiving the adoration and worship of the masses. Elijah Mvundura challenges the sweeping claims of Pope Gregory VII:

> And the claims Gregory VII made in *Dictatus Papae* [twenty-seven statements of power seized by the pope] are radical and heretical. To cite only four: "all princes shall kiss the feet of the Pope alone"—*angels refused human homage* (Revelation 19:10). "His name alone [the pope] shall be spoken in the churches"—*displaced Jesus.* That he can "depose emperors"— *only God can depose or set up kings* (Daniel 2:21), and that "the Roman Church has never erred. Nor will it err, to all eternity"—*Paul's pastoral letters and the letters to the seven churches in the book of Revelation shows that the church errs.* To say otherwise is to arrogate an attribute—*infallibility*— exclusive to God. Indeed, the universal supremacy in religion and in politics claimed by the *Dictatus Papae*, no king, priest, prophet, or apostle ever claimed them in the Bible. It belongs to God alone.[9]

Just over five hundred years ago, one lone monk dared to set out to challenge that brazen assumption of divine power and deception.

"The coming of the lawless one will be in accordance with how Satan works. He will use all sorts of displays of power through signs and wonders that serve the lie, and all the ways that wickedness deceives those who are perishing" (2 Thessalonians 2:9, 10).

Did you catch that? Satan will "use all sorts of displays of power through signs and wonders that serve the lie." What lie would that be? How about the first lie he ever told on this planet?

Remember the Garden of Eden and Eve's encounter with "that ancient serpent called the devil" (Revelation 12:9)? Everyone knows the story:

> Now the serpent was more crafty than any of the wild animals the LORD God had made.
>   He said to the woman, "Did God really say, 'You must not eat from any tree in the garden' "? (Genesis 3:1, 2).

If only she had just walked on by, how different the universe would be today! But she made the mistake we all have made when it comes to the hissing serpent's temptations—we stop and argue. If the devil is, as Jesus described him, "a liar and the father of lies" (John 8:44), then stopping to argue with him only advances his lie, does it not?

"Oh no," Eve innocently replied, "we can eat of every single tree in this garden, except for the one you're coiled in right now." She paused. "Because God told us if we eat from *this* tree, we will die."

"Oh, rubbish!" the serpent hissed back. (Now here it comes. Mark it well—the lie that torpedoed humanity.) " '*You will not certainly die,*' the serpent said to the woman" (Genesis 3:4; emphasis added).

> Both history and prophecy are clear. There is a "man of lawlessness" who will rule on Earth, declaring himself to be God and receiving the adoration and worship of the masses.

What is it the children chant? "Liar, liar, pants on fire." Hasn't Jesus warned us, "There is no truth in him. For when he lies, he speaks his native language, for he is a liar and the father of lies" (John 8:44)?

One single lie: "You will not surely die." But over the passing millennia, it has become embedded in nearly every religion and philosophy on this planet. It is Satan's lie that still deceives: "When you die, you don't really die—oh no, you don't. You go to heaven, or you go to hell, or you go to purgatory, or you enter nirvana, or you simply reincarnate. But be clear—you will never die." Clear? It is the most damning and deceiving lie we face. But coming from the father of lies, should we be surprised?

So it is no surprise that when the Creator came to Earth to defeat the devil and liberate humanity, He set about to expose the enemy's "in the beginning" lie about death. Jesus did it when one of His closest friends died.

Everybody knows the story in John 11. A longtime friend of Jesus named Lazarus has fallen deathly ill. And his desperate sisters, Martha and Mary, send an urgent message to Jesus, who is far away, "Lord, the one you love is sick" (John 11:3). The implied message is: "Please come quickly and heal him before he dies." After all, Jesus has healed hundreds of others. He will surely come and heal their brother.

But Jesus, strangely enough, does not hurry to the side of His beloved and very ill friend, Lazarus. In fact, He waits days and then tells His disciples:

> "Our friend Lazarus has fallen asleep; but I am going there to wake him up."
>
> His disciples replied, "Lord, if he sleeps, he will get better." Jesus had been speaking of his death, but his disciples thought he meant natural sleep.
>
> So then he told them plainly, "Lazarus is dead, and for your sake I am glad I was not there, so that you may believe" (John 11:11–14).

Isn't that amazing—to the great Giver of life, death is nothing more than a sleep. "Lazarus has fallen asleep. He is dead. But I'm going to wake him up!"

That's what He said to Martha when He arrived at their home village of Bethany days later: "I am the resurrection and the life. He who believes in Me, though he may die, he shall live. And whoever lives and believes in Me shall never die [forever]. Do you believe this?" (John 11:25, 26, NKJV).

Lazarus obviously died—but not forever. Why? Because, for the beloved Life-Giver, *death is nothing more than a sleep*, a sleep from which you and I will be awakened when Jesus returns on that glorious resurrection morning!

How long does death last for the one who dies? It lasts this long: Do it with me right now—close your eyes and then immediately open them again. Do it again. What's the point? That is how long death lasts: eyes close in death—and then in what feels like a split second later—eyes open in resurrection. From the last moment of cognition before death to the first moment of cognition at the resurrection—eyes close, eyes open. That is the Bible truth about death.

We all know what it's like for our heads to hit the pillow after an exhausting day, and the next conscious moment we have is that crazy alarm clock beeping to wake us up. That is the sleep of death. Like a baby in their mother's arms, when you die, you will sleep in the arms of God. Seventy times Jesus and the Bible writers describe death as a sleep from which you can be awakened. Satan is a liar. The truth is: when you die, you don't go to heaven or hell or purgatory—*you go to sleep in the arms of God.*

"Yes, but who cares—what's the big deal about what happens when you die?" you may ask.

Fair question.

The biggest and most significantly urgent reason the Bible's truth about death as a sleep is critical today is because of the three ugly green frogs—those "demonic spirits" that come out of the dragon, the sea beast, and the earth beast to perform signs to deceive "the whole world" (Revelation 16:14). And what are those signs? Something visible to deceive you.

Think for a moment. Can you imagine how convincing it would be for our deceased loved ones to appear in the night by our bedsides—beloved mothers, fathers, spouses, and children? "Mommy, Jesus wanted me to come and tell you . . . I'm all right . . . I'm in heaven with Him . . . and I will bring you another message from Him in a few days . . . I love you, Mommy."

Why, what dear mother wouldn't be wild with grief and joy to contact her deceased child again? You don't think the fallen Satan is capable of such deceptions impersonating the dead?

In fact, he has already set the table! There is a website that advertises itself as the SoulPhone Foundation.[10] Scrolling across its home page are these three taglines: "Bringing spirit communication to life," "Ground-breaking technology to contact whose who have passed on," and "Scientific technology for communicating with postmaterial ('deceased') persons." Scroll down the home page; you will read: "What would it mean if you could communicate with 'departed' loved ones and learn from scientists, great teachers, and others who have passed on but definitely not passed away?"[11]

It turns out SoulPhone Foundation is an evidently earnest and serious collaboration of scientists, academics, mediums, and psychologists devoted to establishing connection and proving the existence of deceased "postmaterial persons." Through a device they have created called the

Plasma Globe System, these researchers provide a "switch" for "post-material collaborators (so-called deceased persons involved in the experiment) to signal yes/no to basic questions [posed by the researchers]."[12] Using these measured responses from "the deceased persons" participating in this study, the researchers have already concluded the following:

> The totality of the replicated findings makes it very clear that:
> 1. life continues after bodily death.
> 2. postmaterial collaborators were able to generate accurate 'yes/no' [*sic*] responses during multiple Operator Skills, Cognitive Understanding, and Personal Identification tests.[13]

How do we know the responses of the "postmaterial collaborators" are accurate? Obviously, surviving family members were able to verify the veracity of the "deceased" people's responses. Read some of the lengthy material posted on this website, and you cannot help but sense the eagerness of these academics and scientists to prove their hypothesis to the world: that when you die, you don't really die—you go on living as a "postmaterial" being.

Sound familiar? But should we be surprised? "And no wonder, for Satan himself masquerades as an angel of light. It is not surprising, then, if his servants [angel demons] also masquerade as servants of righteousness [beings of light from heaven]" (2 Corinthians 11:14, 15).

Now imagine "demonic spirits" as described in Revelation 16:14 appearing as "postmaterial collaborators" across the Earth with their sophisticated, heartrending abilities to masquerade as our loved ones, down to the most intimate detail only we could possibly know (e.g., an endearing phrase or some shared private memory). How quickly such "signs" could elicit the exclamations, "That has to be my child," "That has to be my girlfriend," "This must be my mother." Three ugly green frogs, "demonic spirits" pretending to be our loved ones who are sleeping in death.

Why, the potential list of demonic impersonations could be staggering! Struggling global leaders, faced with devastating calamities, are suddenly visited by "postmaterial collaborators" like Winston Churchill or John F. Kennedy. What political leader wouldn't be relieved to receive counsel from deceased superheroes like these? What about now-dead religious leaders such as Pope John Paul II or Billy Graham appearing to confused humanity?

One more line from the SoulPhone Foundation website caught my eye: "A *paradigm shift* will occur after worldwide announcements that afterlife has been scientifically proven. We are doing everything we can to make this shift as positive and comforting as possible."[14] A global paradigm shift? Isn't that precisely what the Apocalypse is predicting? "They are demonic spirits that perform signs, and they go out to the kings of the whole world, to gather them for the battle on the great day of God Almighty" (Revelation 16:14). A global paradigm shift, indeed!

Look, if Jesus is telling the truth—death is a sleep from which He will awaken us at the resurrection—then the "postmaterial collaborators" who are skillfully answering the researchers' questions through plasma signaling are nothing more than fallen angels, demonic spirits impersonating the dead and deceiving the living! That means the "Marian apparitions," as people are calling them—these appearances of mother Mary in various places on Earth—cannot be mother Mary, not if what her Son taught us about death is true. Evil forces are spreading out across the Earth, preparing (and softening up) humanity for the final onslaught. The biblical evidence is both clear and convincing.[15]

> A human's only safety in the face of such withering demonic attacks is Holy Scripture.

Where shall we turn then to prevent ourselves from being duped and deceived by these demonic impostors? "And when they say to you, 'Seek those who are mediums and wizards, who whisper and mutter,' should not a people seek their God? Should they seek the dead on behalf of the living? To the law and to the testimony! If they do not speak according to this word, it is because there is no light in them" (Isaiah 8:19, 20, NKJV). A human's only safety in the face of such withering demonic attacks is holy Scripture. If these deceptive demonic manifestations, if infuriated church prelates attempt to threaten you into submission, your refuge and safety will be where Jesus found His when He was under satanic attack in His wilderness temptations: "It is written" (Matthew 4:4)! Stand on the Word of God and nowhere else. As the old gospel song still sings:

> All other ground is sinking sand,
> All other ground is sinking sand.[16]

Just over five hundred years ago, Martin Luther championed what became the great Protestant principle of *sola scriptura*—"Holy Scripture alone." If they cannot prove it between the covers of your Bible, do not believe it. That is our Protestant legacy. But tragically, the largest and most influential Protestant nation on Earth is drifting further and further from sola scriptura truth. So far that these startling words in *The Great Controversy* are a warning:

> Through the two great errors, the immortality of the soul and Sunday sacredness, Satan will bring the people under his deceptions. While the former lays the foundation of spiritualism [the belief the dead become living spirits], the latter creates a bond of sympathy with Rome. The Protestants of the United States will be foremost in stretching their hands across the gulf to grasp the hand of spiritualism; they will reach over the abyss to clasp hands with the Roman power; and under the influence of this threefold union [the satanic trinity], this country will follow in the steps of Rome in trampling on the rights of conscience.[17]

Remember those words of Mark Noll at the beginning of this chapter? "On the basis of the ecumenical dialogues, can it be said that the Reformation is over? Probably not. But *a once-yawning chasm has certainly narrowed.*"[18] Mark Noll is more right than he may realize. His observation that "a once-yawning chasm has certainly narrowed" is matched by Ellen White's prediction that American Protestants will stretch "their hands across the gulf" to spiritism and the occult and "reach over the abyss" to Rome to form the endgame trinity of darkness. *Chasm, gulf, abyss*—the reality is obvious. Thus the question is not *if* this will come to pass. The question is *when* this will come to pass. Because with each passing day, it becomes clearer *you can get there from here.*

Through the long midnight, he pours out his soul to his Lord. And when the day dawns, it rises upon a man whose worn knees and clinging faith have laid hold upon the Divine.

America! America!
God shed His grace on thee,

And crown thy good with brotherhood
From sea to shining sea.[19]

We must pray for America and stand for Jesus right now.

Alone that April night in his dark and tiny hotel room in the ancient city of Worms, Martin Luther collapses to the cold wooden floor. Seized with an icy fear, his "faith becomes faint; his enemies seem to multiply before him; his imagination is overpowered. . . . His soul is like a ship tossed by a violent tempest, now plunged to the depths of the sea, and again mounting up towards heaven."[20] Well he knows the next day he must appear again before that august assemblage of imperial and ecclesiastical royalty, convened by none other than the young emperor Charles V. But this time there can be no hesitancy, no matter how intimidating the court before which Luther must defend his writings and faith in holy Scripture. So now he presses his anguished face to the earth, and his sobs rend the black night.

The Reformation historian d'Aubigne recounted those cries: " 'God Almighty! God Eternal! how terrible is the world! how it opens its mouth to swallow me up! . . . O Lord! be my help! Faithful God, immutable God! I trust not in any man. . . . Thou hast chosen me for this work. I know it! Act, then, O God! . . . Stand by my side, for the sake of thy well beloved Son Jesus Christ, who is my defence, my buckler, and my fortress.' "[21]

Through the long midnight, he pours out his soul to his Lord. And when the day dawns, it rises upon a man whose worn knees and clinging faith have laid hold upon the Divine. Finally ushered that late afternoon, April 17, 1521, back into the judicial chambers of the Diet, Luther stands once again before the emperor's court. Without a trace of fear or embarrassment, this young pastor and priest launches into a grueling defense of his faith in holy Scripture and his humble efforts to publish the truth he has discovered therein.

Exhausted, he finishes his defense, only to have the magistrates call him to repeat it, this time in Latin. So it was that Providence ordained a twin defense that fated day in court, first in German and then in Latin. Finally, at the end of the wearying day, when Luther is once more grilled, "Will you, or will you not, retract?" he calmly replies:

> "Since your most serene Majesty, and your high Mightinesses, call upon me for a simple, clear, and definite answer, I will give it; and it is this: I cannot subject my faith either to the pope or

to councils, because it is clear as day that they have often fallen into error, and even into great self-contradiction. If, then, I am not disproved by passages of Scripture, or by clear arguments; if I am not convinced by the very passages which I have quoted, and so bound in conscience to submit to the word of God, *I neither can nor will retract any thing*, for it is not safe for a Christian to speak against his conscience."[22]

Facing the assembly for the last time, Luther declares in words still remembered in Protestant homes the world over, " 'Here I stand. I can do no other. God help me! Amen.' "[23]

On the authority of the same holy Scriptures Luther defended, is it not high time for a new generation of protestors to declare to America, to the world, their own "Here I stand" for the Lord Jesus and His Word? You must be one of these. So must I. God help us! Amen.

---

1. Mark Noll, *Is the Reformation Over? An Evangelical Assessment of Contemporary Roman Catholicism* (Grand Rapids, MI: Baker Academic, 2005), 114; emphasis added.

2. Laura M. Fabrycky, "Throwing Ink at the Devil: On Hidden, Creative Labors," Culture Keeper, October 31, 2017, http://www.culture-keeper.com/blog/throwing-ink-at-the-devil-on-hidden-creative-labors.

3. From his German translation of the Bible, Luther chose the opening words of Psalm 46—"*Ein' feste burg ist unser Gott*" (in English, "God is our refuge and strength")—to be the opening line of his great hymn (in English, "A mighty fortress is our God"). Not only was it the battle hymn of the Protestant Reformation, but it is also today the national hymn of Germany. Sung at Luther's funeral, its familiar opening German words are chiseled on his tombstone. See Wayne Hooper and Edward White, *Companion to the Seventh-day Adventist Hymnal* (Hagerstown, MD: Review and Herald®, 1988), 490.

4. Martin Luther, "A Mighty Fortress," tr. Frederick H Hedge (1852).

5. Ranko Stefanovic, *Plain Revelation* (Berrien Springs, MI: Andrews University Press, 2013), 161.

6. Stefanovic, 163, 164.

7. Pope Leo XIII, Encyclical Letter "On the Chief Duties of Christians as Citizens," January 10, 1890, translated in *The Great Encyclical Letters of Pope Leo XIII* (New York: Benziger, 1903), 304, quoted in Howard Peth, *7 Mysteries Solved* (Washington, DC: Hart Books, 2002), 665.

8. Pope Leo XIII, in an encyclical letter dated June 20, 1894, translated in *The Great Encyclical Letters of Pope Leo XIII* (New York: Benziger, 1902), 193, quoted in Peth, *7 Mysteries Solved*, 665.

9. Elijah Mvundura, "Was Medieval Christendom Christian?," *Liberty*, January/February 2021, 26; emphasis in original.

10. SoulPhone Foundation, accessed June 11, 2021, https://www.soulphonefoundation.org.

11. SoulPhone Foundation.

12. Mark Pitstick, "2021 SoulPhone Project Update," SoulPhone Foundation, accessed June 11, 2021, https://www.thesoulphonefoundation.org/soulphone-update/.

13. Pitstick.

14. Pitstick.

15. In my book *Countdown to the Showdown*, there is the following summation of the biblical evidence regarding the true nature of death: "The immortality of the human soul has not a contextual shred of evidence in the entire Scriptures. It is simply a lie. And Lucifer knows it. The 'soul' and 'spirit' of human beings are referred to over 1,700 times in the Bible but are never once said to be immortal or eternal. In fact, the Bible clearly states that only God is immortal (1 Timothy 6:14–16). The spirit that returns to God at death is not a conscious entity, but is the breath of life (Ecclesiastes 12:7; Genesis 2:7). The words *spirit*, *wind*, and *breath* in our English translations come the same original Hebrew and Greek words in the Bible. The Bible says the dead cannot remember or give thanks (Psalm 6:5), cannot praise God (Psalm 115:7; Isaiah 38:18), cannot think (Psalm 146:3, 4), and cannot function (Ecclesiastes 9:5, 6, 10). Their abode is the grave, not heaven (Acts 2:29, 34)." Dwight K. Nelson, *Countdown to the Showdown* (Fallbrook, CA: Hart Research Center, 1992), 96.

16. Edward Mote, "My Hope Is Built on Nothing Less" (1834).

17. Ellen G. White, *The Great Controversy* (Mountain View, CA: Pacific Press®, 1950), 588.

18. Noll, *Is the Reformation Over?*, 114; emphasis added.

19. Katharine Lee Bates, "America the Beautiful" (1893).

20. Jean-Henri Merle d'Aubigne, *History of the Reformation in the Sixteenth Century*, vol. 2 (Glasgow, UK: William Collins, 1846), book 7, chapter 8, http://www.gutenberg.org/files/41470/41470-h/41470-h.htm#CHAP_VIII7.

21. d'Aubigne.

22. d'Aubigne.

23. James M. Kittelson, *Luther the Reformer: The Story of the Man and His Career* (Minneapolis, MN: Fortress Press, 2003), 161.

The Assyrian Empire was the baddest

of the bad, and yet God spared it the

destruction its atrocities deserved. So

if God can forgive Nineveh and save its

political leader, could He not also revive

America and save our political leaders?

CAN GOD REVIVE AMERICA?

Here's the million-dollar question for you and me: Can God revive America? One of our Canadian viewers sent me an article from the Canadian Broadcasting Corporation News website entitled "Things Fall Apart in the United States—and Canada Takes a Hard Look in the Mirror." News journalist Aaron Wherry writes: "The United States has offered the world a demonstration of how things can fall apart—not in one cataclysmic moment, but slowly and steadily over a long period of time as institutions and ideas erode and crumble."[1] Like the Roman Empire, do you suppose?

Can God revive America? A group of us got together the other night for a Zoom prayer meeting focused on America. And I was moved when a friend of mine took us to the book of Jonah. And all he did was read these verses aloud. I say we do the same:

> Then the word of the LORD came to Jonah a second time: "Go to the great city of Nineveh and proclaim to it the message I give you."
>
> Jonah obeyed the word of the LORD and went to Nineveh. Now Nineveh was a very large city; it took three days to go through it. Jonah began by going a day's journey into the city, proclaiming, "Forty more days and Nineveh will be overthrown." The Ninevites believed God. A fast was proclaimed, and all of them, from the greatest to the least, put on sackcloth.
>
> When Jonah's warning reached the king of Nineveh, he rose from his throne, took off his royal robes, covered himself with sackcloth and sat down in the dust. This is the proclamation he issued in Nineveh:
>
> "By the decree of the king and his nobles:

> Do not let people or animals, herds or flocks, taste anything;
> do not let them eat or drink. But let people and animals be
> covered with sackcloth. Let everyone call urgently on God.
> Let them give up their evil ways and their violence. Who
> knows? God may yet relent and with compassion turn from
> his fierce anger so that we will not perish."
>
> When God saw what they did and how they turned from
> their evil ways, he relented and did not bring on them the
> destruction he had threatened (Jonah 3:1–10).

Can you believe that? The Assyrian Empire was the baddest of the bad, and yet God spared it the destruction its atrocities deserved. So if God can forgive Nineveh and save its political leader, could He not also revive America and save our political leaders?

Let's ask the question another way: Can *we* revive America? Too obvious an answer? I'm not so sure. In all candor, I am amazed at some solutions coming from some educated circles about how to advance God's kingdom in America.

In the *Christianity Today* podcast *Quick to Listen*, host Morgan Lee interviews Kim Colby, a graduate of Harvard Law School and now with the Christian Legal Society's Center for Law and Religious Freedom. They talked about the appointment of Amy Coney Barrett to the United States Supreme Court in the fall of 2020. Along the way, the two note how "Coney Barrett's relationship with her Catholic-Charismatic community, People of Praise, has drawn scrutiny as critics have asked what type of authority this group might have over her judicial decisions."[2]

From a transcript of this interview posted on the *Christianity Today* website, these lines caught my eye:

> LEE: "Generally speaking, Protestants and Catholics read
> the Bible differently, so do you think that they would also
> have different feelings about [how to read and interpret the
> Constitution] as a result?"
>
> COLBY: "Well, that is interesting. I haven't thought about
> it myself or really explored it. My instinct would be no [they
> would not read the Constitution differently], even though
> because theologically, that's true [they do read the Bible
> differently]."[3]

Then—and this is what caught my eye—Colby related a debate at Harvard last summer: "There is a divide very recently where a Catholic law professor at Harvard came out and said, *when we have the political power to impose what's right as we understand our faith to teach what's right, then we should do that.*"[4]

That's one way to have a revival in America—legislate it! *"When we have the political power to impose what's right as we understand our faith to teach what's right, then we should do that."*

COLBY: "And I don't agree with that. I think it's a very dangerous idea. And there was a lot of debate about that for a few weeks this summer."[5]

Dangerous indeed, because who decides whose faith it is that needs to be legislated? Is it the Roman Catholic's faith? The Baptist's faith? The Presbyterian's faith? The Seventh-day Adventist's faith? Who decides whose faith is the right interpretation of the faith? The answer is obvious—whoever has the most votes. How else are you going to decide the correct faith to legislate?

But imagine that scenario for a moment. With all the bedlam in this country over counting ballots this past election, can you envision what it would be like getting a roomful of clergy and politicians together to try to decide whose faith is the right faith to legislate? And then vote on it? Deliver us!

But don't miss the subsidiary point. The only way a "voted faith" can pass is if its adherents constitute the majority of voters (be it in a legislative committee or a statehouse or Congress). And the moment the majority decides, what happens to the minority? Just look at what happened to the minorities down through the dark ages of Christendom. Not sure? Trust me—they were "voted off the island," or more factually, decimated out of the land. No, when it comes to matters of the heart and faith and religion, majority vote is the death knell of minority faith.

"When we have the political power to impose what's right as we understand our faith to teach what's right, then we should do that." The Catholic Harvard professor made his point clearly enough. But he is clearly wrong. You will never revive America by legislative majority or popular vote.

But can *God* revive America? There is a single line in the Apocalypse that promises that before this endgame is over, God will ignite a mighty spiritual, moral revival, the likes of which this nation and planet have never witnessed.

> After this I saw another angel coming down from heaven. He had great authority, and the earth was illuminated by his splendor (Revelation 18:1).

Have you seen those screen saver videos shot by drones or satellites with breathtaking vistas of Earth from high in the sky? I downloaded some onto my Mac laptop. And they are so fascinating that I drop whatever I'm doing just to watch. Have you seen the one that is a night shot of this country? Go to Google right now and click on this NASA satellite photograph of America at night.[6] You are gazing on this "God Bless America" land, spread out in the darkness, its towns and cities captured as tiny pinpoints of light or yellow ponds of urban spread. The good news is that what the Apocalypse just described for us is not only the United States but the entire planet set ablaze by pinpoints of celestial light.

> After this I saw another angel coming down from heaven. He had great authority, and the earth was illuminated by his splendor (Revelation 18:1).

The good news is that what the Apocalypse just described for us is not only the United States but the entire planet set ablaze by pinpoints of celestial light.

So whose glory is this in Revelation 18? It is the glory of the Lord Jesus, of course. Whoever this high-ranking angel is—think of him as the fourth angel after the three angels in Revelation 14—he is simply reflecting the glory of Someone else. Because angels, like humans, have a glory derived not from within but from without. We are like the moon—the only reason it brightens the night sky is that it beautifully reflects the glory of the sun.

Nearly every line in Revelation is either a direct quote from or an echo or allusion to an Old Testament passage. And Revelation 18:1 is no exception: "Afterward he brought me to the gate, the gate that faces toward the east [the Hebrew word for *east* is "the place of the sunrise"].

And behold, the glory of the God of Israel came from the way of the east [the prophet is describing that sunrise, slowly peeking higher and higher on the eastern horizon]. His voice was like the sound of many waters; *and the earth shone with His glory*" (Ezekiel 43:1, 2, NKJV; emphasis added).

Ezekiel's last line here is a direct connection with Revelation 18:1: "And the earth was illuminated with his glory" (NKJV). So now we know the glory that bathes the earth in the endgame's explosion of light is the glory of the God of Israel, as Ezekiel described Him. And what is more, Ezekiel adds, "His voice was like the sound of many waters" (Ezekiel 43:2, NKJV). Which, as it turns out, are the very words of John's eyewitness-earwitness account of Jesus' personal theophany to the elderly disciple there on the rocky Isle of Patmos: "And His voice [was] the sound of many waters" (Revelation 1:15, NKJV).

So the inescapable conclusion is the glory that bursts across the earth like the rising sun during the endgame of the Apocalypse is none other than the glory of the Lord Jesus Christ Himself. But then, is anyone surprised the book known as the Revelation of Jesus Christ would depict the last moments of history as a glorious sunburst of the Sun of Righteousness enveloping this planet just before the end of time? Why, even the last book of the Old Testament affirms the same: "But for you who revere my name, the sun of righteousness will rise with healing in its rays" (Malachi 4:2).[7] A "Sonrise" indeed![8]

So what is transpiring here in Revelation 18? Clearly, it is not the Second Coming. That's the spectacular theme of Revelation 19. Something else is afoot. Or rather could it be *Someone* else is afoot? What we know thus far is Revelation 18:1 depicts some sort of global heavenly intervention. An angelic ambassador, who obviously streaks earthward from the very throne room of Christ—how else does this angelic being radiate the glory of Jesus?—descends to Earth with a message of sonic-booming power at the end of time, though not quite the end:

> After this I saw another angel coming down from heaven. He had great authority, and the earth was illuminated by his splendor. With a mighty voice he shouted:
>
> " 'Fallen! Fallen is Babylon the Great!' "
> She has become a dwelling for demons
> and a haunt for every impure spirit" (Revelation 18:1, 2).

It is curtains for the dragon and his Earth surrogates, the sea beast and the earth beast. But before the final curtain falls, Almighty God Himself, "who was, and is, and is to come" (Revelation 4:8), steps onto the battlefield and in that explosion of glory seizes the initiative and launches a spiritual offensive not seen since the halcyon days of long ago Pentecost. The Divine One, who better than any other, lives by the adage "Go big or go home," now goes *big*—because this is the last revival ever to take place on this planet before the end.

But is anybody surprised? Look at how He did it in the beginning:

> When the day of Pentecost came, they were all together in one place. Suddenly a sound [note that this is not the physical movements of a gale-force wind, but the roaring *sound* of a cyclone wind] like the blowing of a violent wind came from heaven and filled the whole house where they were sitting. They saw what seemed to be tongues of fire that separated [the Greek describes a fiery ball from which are peeled, like peeling an orange, slices of fiery peelings or tongues] and came to rest on each of them. All of them were filled with the Holy Spirit and began to speak in other tongues [the NIV's margin notes the word *languages*] as the Spirit enabled them (Acts 2:1–4).

Such an explosive invasion of the mighty Spirit of God could not be concealed in that upper room above the alleyways of Jerusalem. Word of this mysterious outpouring spread like wildfire, and soon literally thousands of citizens were swelling the streets of the ancient city. "Then Peter stood up with the Eleven, raised his voice [multiple decibels for sure] and addressed the crowd" (Acts 2:14). He quotes the ancient prophecy of Joel, and either he or Luke, who much later recorded this event in Acts, under the inspiration of the Holy Spirit, added the words "in the last days" (Acts 2:17). And that simple but noteworthy inclusion catapults the significance of both Joel's ancient prophecy and this Pentecost manifestation to our day. Here are the words Peter quoted:

> In the last days, God says,
>   I will pour out my Spirit on all people.
> Your sons and daughters will prophesy,
>   your young men will see visions,
>   your old men will dream dreams.

Even on my servants, both men and women,
I will pour out my Spirit in those days,
and they will prophesy.
I will show wonders in the heavens above
and signs on the earth below,
blood and fire and billows of smoke.
The sun will be turned to darkness
and the moon to blood
before the coming of the great and glorious day of the Lord.
And everyone who calls
on the name of the Lord will be saved (Acts 2:17–21).

Did you get that? What Peter actually describes is an end-time ("in the last days") outpouring of the Holy Spirit "on all people," irrespective of age, gender, or social class. A spiritual wildfire, a divine unleashing of glory so civilization-penetrating that even nature itself is upturned "before the coming of the great and glorious day of the Lord"! Yes, Pentecost was the spectacular visible launching of the story and mission of Christ through His church. But can we even fathom how this same Jesus and this same church at the end of time will visibly, triumphantly bring down the final curtain?

After this I saw another angel coming down from heaven. He had great authority, and the earth was illuminated by his splendor (Revelation 18:1).

This apocalyptic explosion of glory across the raging spiritual battlefield of Earth will be the dramatic coup d'état of the mighty Third Person of the Divine Trinity over and against the confederated forces of the satanic trinity. As it was in the beginning, the dramatic world triumph of truth in the end not only penetrates the hemorrhaging darkness of falsehood and error but also collapses the confederacy of evil into a tragedy of self-destruction. "Fallen, fallen is Babylon the Great!" (Revelation 18:2, NRSV).

The apocalyptic classic *The Great Controversy* describes the spiritual magnitude of the last Sonrise:

The [fourth] angel who unites in the proclamation of the third angel's message is to lighten the whole earth with his glory

[Revelation 18:1]. A work of world-wide extent and unwonted [extraordinary] power is here foretold. . . .

The great work of the gospel is not to close with less mani-festation of the power of God than marked its opening.[9]

Pentecost we can picture because history and inspiration have preserved the opening saga and stories of Jesus' church. But how shall we imagine the ending to the same church, the eventual story up close and personal? Consider this graphic depiction:

Servants of God [friends of Jesus], with their faces lighted up and shining [they have obviously gotten close to Jesus[10]] with holy consecration, will hasten from place to place [what this generation can do so well—all we need is a laptop, plane ticket, and passport—and we're gone!] to proclaim the message from heaven. By thousands of voices, all over the earth, the warning will be given [e.g., "Jesus is coming soon, so turn back from the darkness to the light of His truth"]. Miracles will be wrought, the sick will be healed, and signs and wonders will follow the believers. [But not to be left out] Satan also works, with lying wonders, [the devil is not going to stand by and let this global revival rain on his parade] even bringing down fire from heaven in the sight of men. Revelation 13:13. Thus the inhabitants of the earth will be brought to take their stand.[11]

Revelation 18:1 is no dress rehearsal or some cheap imitation. It is the real deal—a genuine global revival the likes of which earnest followers of Christ have been pleading for through the centuries. The Bible calls it the "latter rain," the last apocalyptic rainfall of the Holy Spirit on the human race: "Therefore be patient, [friends], until the coming of the Lord. See how the farmer waits for the precious fruit of the earth, waiting patiently for it until it receives the early and latter rain" (James 5:7, NKJV).[12] Pentecost was the mighty early, or first, rain of the Holy Spirit upon the church. But Revelation 18:1 portends an even mightier latter, or last, rain.

Norman Gulley refers to this apocalyptic outpouring of God's Spirit as "the second coming of the Holy Spirit."[13] Pentecost was the early rain, or "first coming," and the Revelation 18:1 apocalyptic outpouring (the latter rain) is the "second coming." And Gulley's premise is quite simple and direct. If you want to be ready for the second coming of Jesus, you must first experience the second coming of the Holy Spirit.

Does that make sense? Remember Jesus' parable of the ten girlfriends, who had all been invited to a wedding but who all fell asleep waiting for the delayed bridegroom to come?[14] Eventually, the cry goes out, "He's coming!" But when the ten young women awaken, five of them realize they ran out of oil for their lamps while they were sleeping (when Jesus told the story, Middle Eastern weddings often were a nighttime event). "Give us some of your oil; our lamps are going out," they begged their five girlfriends (Matthew 25:8). But there wasn't enough to go around, so the five foolish girlfriends hurried off at midnight to procure more oil and thus missed the coming of the bridegroom. They missed it all because they didn't have the daily fresh oil of the Spirit of Jesus in their lives.

Norman Gulley writes: "Here's the bottom line: To be ready for the second coming of Christ we must be ready for the second coming of the Holy Spirit. But to be unready for the coming of the Holy Spirit is to be unready for the coming of Christ."[15] That is, to take Jesus' second coming seriously necessitates taking seriously the second coming of the Holy Spirit, which must by necessity precede the return of Jesus. Thus, Gulley warns those who presume it is enough simply to be a member of a church: "Remember, some members wait for the latter rain to prepare them for heaven, only to find it's too late."[16] Remember the five foolish girlfriends.

Revelation 18:1 depicts the mighty and promised second coming of the Holy Spirit. But to ignore the mounting evidence of Christ's soon coming and to presume there will be a great revival one day that will make us ready is to remain unready.

Will God revive America? The Apocalypse assures its readers the *whole world* will be brightened one day with the glory of the Spirit of Christ poured out on people eager to be filled with Jesus. But genuine revivals remain hard to come by these days.

Because the truth is the dragon is no dummy, and the rebel angel Satan knows these apocalyptic prophecies better than we do. Why would he want a single human being to experience the real deal of that end-time outpouring of Holy Spirit power? Why, if I were him, I would scramble to concoct false revivals all over the earth, counterfeit revivings that would appear to be genuine but would be seductively embedded with the dragon's own falsehoods, Satan's carefully crafted counterfeits to the Creator and His truth. Look, if the dragon and his cohorts can "even [cause] fire to come from heaven to the earth in full view of the people" (Revelation 13:13), could he not ignite a "fake fire" of emotional highs, of counterfeit signs and wonders in churches across the land?

Jesus, in His beloved sermon on the mount, warned about "fake fire": "Not everyone who says to me, 'Lord, Lord,' will enter the kingdom of heaven, but only the one who does the will of my Father who is in heaven. Many will say to me on that day, 'Lord, Lord, did we not prophesy in your name and in your name drive out demons and in your name perform many miracles?' Then I will tell them plainly, 'I never knew you. Away from me, you evildoers!' " (Matthew 7:21–23). Miracles and prophecies and exorcisms, all done in the name of Jesus, can apparently turn out to be grist for a false revival that will not stand the test of time nor the test of our Lord Himself. What was Jesus' test for revivals? "Only the one who does the will of my Father who is in heaven" "will enter the kingdom of heaven" (Matthew 7:21). Plain and simple, radical obedience to God and His word is the test of genuine revival. To reject the Creator's day of worship for the more convenient substitute offered by the satanic trinity and yet boast of revival is a sure sign of the inauthenticity of that revival.

Consider for a moment the Pentecostal-charismatic movement that has swept the world today. "There were 981,000 of these souls in 1900; there are 643,661,000 of them today; and there are projected to be over one billion Charismatics and Pentecostals in 2050. In raw numbers, then, Charismatic and Pentecostal Christianity is the fastest growing phenomenon in world religious history."[17]

Of course, there are sincere Christians who belong to this movement, people honestly seeking to follow Jesus and obey His truth. But the very nature of their sincerity will mean an open-minded heart when they discover further and deeper truths in holy Scripture. The danger of the Pentecostal-charismatic movement and practice is that its dominantly emotion-focused experience has tended to block or short-circuit a biblically and intellectually faithful obedience to countercultural Bible teachings they dismiss as either inconvenient or too doctrinal for their easy-belief brand of Christianity.

Ron Clouzet tells of a woman caller to a radio talk-show pastor who apparently was challenging her charismatic beliefs and practice. He writes that she responded, " 'You resort to Greek translations and fancy words to explain away what the Holy Spirit is doing in the church today.' " She took a breath and continued, " 'Let me give you a piece of advice that might just save you from the wrath of Almighty God: Put away your Bible and your books and stop studying. Ask the Holy Ghost to come upon you and give you the gift of tongues. You have no right to question something you have never experienced.' "[18]

Walter Hollenweger, an authority on the ecumenical movement, identifies the influence the Pentecostal-charismatic movement has had in uniting Christian communions:

> The uniqueness of the charismatic renewal [is] in the fact that for the first time since the Reformation, an Ecumenical grass roots has emerged which has crossed the frontiers between Evangelicals and Catholics. This indeed is of great significance. The basis of this ecumenical approach is the fact that Christians have discovered a common experience, which is at the heart of their spirituality—and this, in spite of their differing theologies and interpretations of this experience.[19]

Of course, it would be wonderful for the Christian communities of Earth to unite. But on what basis would unity be defined and achieved? Holy Scripture knows of only one foundation for lasting unity. Jesus prayed it for His disciples on the eve of His crucifixion:

Holy Father, protect them by the power of your name, the name you gave me, so that they may be one as we are one.

. . . Sanctify them by the truth; *your word is truth* (John 17:11, 17; emphasis added).

To be one as Christ and His Father are one can be our Christian experience only on the basis of His word of truth. Ecumenical unity based on charismatic experience will never rise to Jesus' definition of unity. His prayer "that they may be one" presupposes our allegiance and obedience to the holy Scripture of our Holy Father. Unity based on anything less than obedience to the Word of God is not unity at all but simply political or social convenience.

For us all, the warning of Jesus is critical: "Not everyone who says to me, 'Lord, Lord,' will enter the kingdom of heaven, but only the one who does the will of my Father who is in heaven" (Matthew 7:21).

And that is the only way God will be able to revive America today. Or tomorrow. There can be no lasting personal or collective revival apart from the radical obedience to Jesus' commands of His followers.

Reflecting on the global revival Revelation 18:1 depicts, *The Great Controversy* offers this hopeful perspective:

Notwithstanding the widespread declension of faith and piety, there are true followers of Christ in these churches [across America]. Before the final visitation of God's judgments upon the earth there will be among the people of the Lord such a revival of primitive godliness as has not been witnessed since apostolic times. The Spirit and power of God will be poured out upon His children. At that time many will separate themselves from those churches in which the love of this world has supplanted love for God and His word. Many, both of ministers and people, will gladly accept those great truths which God has caused to be proclaimed at this time to prepare a people for the Lord's second coming.[20]

Good news for America! The mighty Spirit of God will be poured out in "a revival of primitive godliness" (think the book of Acts) unlike any other revival that has swept this nation in its three centuries of religious life. Not even this COVID-19 pandemic can thwart the movings of the Almighty across these "purple mountain majesties above the fruited plains," as the beloved "America the Beautiful" sings.[21] In fact, even the difficult woes and heartbreaking losses of this seemingly unending pandemic may yet open the door to the soul of this nation in ways never imagined, so that the "Spirit and power of God will be poured out upon His children," irrespective of race, gender, socio-economic status, or education. "America! America! God shed His grace on thee."[22] Cannot we pray for the answer to that prayer?

> Unity based on anything less than obedience to the Word of God is not unity at all but simply political or social convenience.

But be forewarned. The often thwarted and raging apocalyptic dragon will yet attempt to seal the heavens to prevent the Spirit's rainfall. *The Great Controversy* warns: "The enemy of souls desires to hinder this work; and before the time for such a movement shall come, he will endeavor to prevent it by introducing a counterfeit. In those churches which he can bring under his deceptive power he will make it appear that God's special blessing is poured out; there will be manifest what is thought to be great religious interest. Multitudes will exult that God is working marvelously for them, when the work is that of another spirit. Under a religious guise, Satan will seek to extend his influence over the Christian world."[23]

All the more reason for us to band together in calling upon God to stir our own hearts, our national soul, that we might yet hear the apocalyptic appeal of Jesus at the door to America's heart:

> Here I am! I stand at the door and knock. If anyone hears my voice and opens the door, I will come in and eat with that person, and they with me (Revelation 3:20).

Can you imagine it? This offer of personal intimacy with the Savior of the world is made to a nation, or at least the people of a nation who pursue unbridled intimacy on so many bankrupted fronts—from experimenting with our sexuality to roaming our social media, from surfing the internet to gaming Wall Street. Millions of us—thirsty for self-worth, personal harmony, economic security, social acceptance, public recognition, and many other comforts—continually turn to the very places and faces that can never slake our deepest thirst.

David Brooks—writer, *New York Times* journalist, political commentator—in his book *The Second Mountain: The Quest for a Moral Life*, details the numbing emptiness young women on the ascendency have confessed:

> Journalist Lisa Miller describes an "ambition collision" she saw in her peers, mostly young women of the professional set. These are the opportunity seizers, she writes, the list makers, the ascendant females weaned on Sheryl Sandberg's *Lean In*, who delayed marriage and children because they were driven to do big things and run big things. But at a certain age, Miller writes, they've "lost it, like a child losing grasp of a helium balloon. Grief-stricken, they are baffled too." As one woman told Miller, "There's no vision." Or, as another put it, there's "nothing solid." They fantasize about quitting their jobs and moving home to Michigan, or having kids merely as an excuse to drop out of the rat race. "They murmur about purpose, about the concrete satisfactions of baking a loaf of bread or watching a garden grow." They stay put, diligently working, "waiting for something—anything—to reignite them, to convince them that their wanting hasn't abandoned them for good."[24]

It's not just America's young women, but America's all of us. Brooks agrees:

> I notice many men also have a sensation that they are under-living their lives. . . .
> . . . It is a lack of care. It is living a life that doesn't arouse your strong passions and therefore instills a sluggishness of the soul, like an oven set on warm. The person . . . may have a job and a family, but he is not entirely grabbed by his own life. His heart is over there, but his life is over here.[25]

To the likes of us with lives so unwell and unlived, Jesus comes knocking: "Would you be willing to open the door and let Me come in? I am what you long for,[26] the relationship you've futilely searched for,[27] contentment that has never arrived,[28] forgiveness for the clinging guilt you've never been able to shed.[29] If you invite Me into your life, I will be your Friend, for I will never abandon you.[30] And believe Me, I am not Someone to be afraid of, I am Someone to be a friend of."[31]

Those hands that knock on the lintel of your life right now are nail-scarred. Did you notice? Hands pinned to that Roman stake and belonging, as the Apocalypse renders it, "to him who loves us [present tense] and has freed us [past tense] from our sins by his blood" (Revelation 1:5). You are already loved and already freed by the Jesus who stands at your door and knocks. You may have let Him in a thousand times before or never once. It matters not to Him. *You* are what matters to the Christ, and if you dare invite Him in, I promise you He will ignite in your soul of souls the very fire to compel you, propel you out of the heavy gloom of your hopelessness into the sunshine glory of the One who promises, "I am making everything new" (Revelation 21:5).

"Yes," you might reply, "but I can't come to Him—look at the mess I've lived." Then I have two pieces of good news just for you. First, it is He who comes to you, not you to Him. "We love Him because He first loved us" (1 John 4:19, NKJV). And second, if you open the door, He will never change His mind: "Oops—wrong house!" This is His promise to you: "Whoever comes to me, I will never [this is a double negative in the Greek: "I will no not ever"] drive away" (John 6:37). Two negatives in case you missed the first one. "I will never, never change My mind and reject you."

I carry with me this stunning quotation, taped in the back of my Bible:

The message from God to me for you is "Him that cometh unto me, I will in no wise cast out" (John 6:37). If you have nothing else to plead before God but this one promise from your Lord and Saviour, you have the assurance that you will never, never [double negative] be turned away. It may seem to you that you are hanging upon a single promise, but appropriate that one promise, and it will open to you the whole treasure house of the riches of the grace of Christ. Cling to that promise and you are safe. "Him that cometh unto me I will in no wise cast out." *Present this assurance to Jesus, and you are as safe as though inside the city of God.*[32]

Does it get any better than that? This promise from Jesus not only opens to you "the whole treasure house of the riches of [His] grace," which would be priceless enough. But hold on to the promise in John 6:37, and it is as if you are already *"inside the city of God"*—which, being interpreted, means *inside heaven itself!* Because with this promise, you have Jesus forever and ever. Amen.

It has been called "the most travelled art work in history."[33] The English artist William Holman Hunt (1827–1910) painted three colorful, allegorical renditions of Jesus as represented in the Apocalypse's depiction: "Here I am! I stand at the door and knock" (Revelation 3:20). Though the words of this text were written beneath the painting, the three extant oil-on-canvas paintings (nearly identical in detail but not in size) became known as the *The Light of the World* (focusing on the light shining upon Jesus' face and the lighted lantern in his hand).

From 1905 to 1907, the third and largest painting went on a world tour and drew crowds by the millions. In fact, in its tour of Australia, it was estimated that four-fifths of the population of the country saw what was called "a sermon in a frame."[34] The painting hangs today in London's St. Paul's Cathedral. (For a screen-size rendition of this painting, follow either link in endnotes 33 or 34.)

There are several pointed details the viewer soon discovers in Holman Hunt's portrayal of Jesus at the heart's door. First, the artist painted no handle or knob on the door. The implication is clear—if the knocking Visitor is to gain entrance, someone on the inside will need to open the door. Second, the doornails and hinges are rusted, and growing around the foot of the door are weeds, with several vines climbing up the exterior of the door. This implication is inescapable—nobody has opened that door in a long, long time.

So how long has it been since the door of your own heart has been opened? A few days? A few years? Never? Can you hear Him knocking now? Why not let this be the time you open the door and invite Him in?

Again, we ask: Can God revive America? The answer is certain: Oh yes, He can. And I happen to believe He will one day. Revive America. One person at a time. And I can't think of one person needier and readier for that revival than you. And me. So why not answer the door and let Jesus in . . . right now? One day at a time—until He comes.

Because you see, a revival happens when multiple people open the doors of their hearts to Jesus at the same time. Then the darkness where they live springs to light. And with enough people opening their hearts' doors to Jesus, you can just imagine how the whole wide world will light up with His glory!

Amen, indeed.

---

1. Aaron Wherry, "Things Fall Apart in the United States—and Canada Takes a Hard Look in the Mirror," CBC News, October 31, 2020, https://www.cbc.ca/news/politics /united-states-trump-biden-democracy-canada-1.5783716.

2. Kim Colby, "Amy Coney Barrett and the Christian Legal Community," interview by Morgan Lee, *Quick to Listen* (podcast), *Christianity Today,* October 13, 2020, https://www .christianitytoday.com/ct/podcasts/quick-to-listen/amy-coney-barrett-christian-law -community-legal-society.html.

3. Colby.

4. Colby; emphasis added.

5. Colby.

6. "NASA-NOAA Satellite Reveals New Views of Earth at Night," NASA, December 5, 2012, https://www.nasa.gov/mission_pages/NPP/news/earth-at-night.html.

7. Malachi 4:1, 5 describe the fiery events of the "day of the LORD" as the eschatological context for this endgame rising of "the sun of righteousness" (Malachi 4:2) over the earth.

8. A Sonrise corroborated by Jesus' own self-description twice when He said, "I am the light of the world" (John 8:12; John 9:5); by Paul's championing this identical portrayal when he wrote, "For God, who said, 'Let light shine out of darkness,' made his light shine in our hearts to give us the light of the knowledge of God's glory displayed in the face of Christ" (2 Corinthians 4:6); and by John's own eyewitness depiction when the risen and ascended Christ appeared to him on Patmos, "His face was like the sun shining in all its brilliance" (Revelation 1:16). Certainly the Apocalypse's predicted end-time sunrise circumnavigating the earth is the Sonrise of Jesus' glory, as Habakkuk himself prophesied: "For the earth will be filled with the knowledge of the glory of the LORD as the waters cover the sea" (Habakkuk 2:14). Sonrise indeed!

9. Ellen G. White, *The Great Controversy* (Mountain View, CA: Pacific Press®, 1950), 611.

10. "And they took note that these men [Peter and John] had been with Jesus" (Acts 4:13).

11. White, *Great Controversy*, 621.

12. The early and latter rain motif reflects farming in Palestine, where the early autumn rains (October–November) softened the soil and enabled the farmer to plant his seed, and the latter or spring rains (March–April) gave a final burst of maturing growth to the grain in preparation for the harvest.

13. Norman Gulley, *Christ Is Coming!* (Hagerstown, MD: Review and Herald®, 1998), 500.

14. See Matthew 25:1–13.

15. Gulley, *Christ Is Coming!*, 500.

16. Gulley, 499.

17. George Weigel, "World Christianity by the Numbers," *First Things*, February 25, 2015, https://www.firstthings.com/web-exclusives/2015/02/world-christianity-by-the-numbers.

18. Ron Clouzet, *Adventism's Greatest Need* (Nampa, ID: Pacific Press®, 2011), 196.

19. Walter Hollenweger, *Pentecostalism: Origins and Developments Worldwide* (Peabody, MA: Hendrickson), 300, quoted in Clouzet, *Adventism's Greatest Need*, 195.

20. White, *Great Controversy*, 464.

21. Katharine Lee Bates, "America the Beautiful" (1893).

22. Bates, "America the Beautiful."

23. White, *Great Controversy*, 494.

24. David Brooks, *The Second Mountain: The Quest for a Moral Life* (New York: Random House, 2019), 23.

25. Brooks, 24.

26. "Whoever drinks the water I give them will never thirst" (John 4:14).

27. "You will seek me and find me when you seek me with all your heart. I will be found by you" (Jeremiah 29:13, 14).

28. "So do not worry, saying, 'What shall we eat?' or 'What shall we drink?' or 'What shall we wear?' For the pagans run after all these things, and your heavenly Father knows that you need them" (Matthew 6:31, 32).

29. "Then neither do I condemn you" (John 8:11), for "the LORD has laid on him the iniquity of us all" (Isaiah 53:6).

30. "Never will I leave you; never will I forsake you" (Hebrews 13:5).

31. "Greater love has no one than this: to lay down one's life for one's friends. You are my friends" (John 15:13, 14).

32. Ellen G. White, *Manuscript Releases*, vol. 10 (Silver Spring, MD: Ellen G. White Estate, 1990), 175; emphasis added.

33. "The Light of the World," St. Paul's Cathedral, accessed June 13, 2021, https://www.stpauls.co.uk/history-collections/the-collections/collections-highlights/the-light-of-the-world.

34. Zelda Caldwell, "This Painting of Jesus Knocking at a Door Is the Most Traveled Work of Art in History," Aleteia, February 7, 2019, https://aleteia.org/2019/02/07/this-painting-of-jesus-knocking-at-a-door-is-the-most-traveled-work-of-art-in-history/.

The sexual revolution of the '60s and '70s

may have sown the wind, but without a

doubt, we are now reaping the whirlwind

of that sexual left turn.

"COME AND DIE"

Nothing relaxes me like a new jigsaw puzzle (five hundred pieces, of course—anything more turns relaxation into interminable work for me). You've got to admit there is a certain satisfaction and even joy in taking what look like utterly disconnected and seemingly unrelated snippets of that striking picture on the box and (slowly) witnessing that colorful vista come into being piece by piece there on the dining room table. What follows are a few more pieces of this stunning apocalyptic vision we've been putting together. And until these pieces are placed carefully into position, the vision is not complete.

Take, for example, the upward trend of the "nones" in this country (those are the Americans who in surveys check the category None in identifying their religious preference). Their rising numbers are well documented and have been much ballyhooed and discussed in both secular and religious media. In a recent *Atlantic* article, "America Without God," Shadi Hamid summarized the reality this nation faces today: "The United States had long been a holdout among Western democracies, uniquely and perhaps even suspiciously devout. From 1937 to 1998, church membership remained relatively constant, hovering at about 70 percent. Then something happened. Over the past two decades, that number has dropped to less than 50 percent, the sharpest recorded decline in American history. Meanwhile, the 'nones'—atheists, agnostics, and those claiming no religion—have grown rapidly and today represent a quarter of the population."[1]

So it should not be surprising that America's Generation Z (today's late teens and twenty-somethings) are in the midst of this national drift toward the "nones." As they began appearing on the radar screen of American demographics, James Emery White described their growing influence on this culture: "Drop everything and start paying attention to Generation Z, which now constitutes 25.9 percent of the US population. . . . By 2020, members of Generation Z will account for 40 percent of all consumers.

They will not simply influence American culture, as any generation would; *they will constitute American culture.*"[2]

And what is Generation Z's religious preference? The Barna Research Group discovered the following:

> It may come as no surprise that the influence of Christianity in the United States is waning. Rates of church attendance, religious affiliation, belief in God, prayer and Bible-reading have been dropping for decades. Americans' beliefs are becoming more post-Christian and, concurrently, religious identity is changing. Enter Generation Z: Born between 1999 and 2015, they are the first truly "post-Christian" generation. More than any other generation before them, Gen Z does not assert a religious identity. They might be drawn to things spiritual, but with a vastly different starting point from previous generations, many of whom received a basic education on the Bible and Christianity. And it shows: *The percentage of Gen Z that identifies as atheist is double that of the U.S. adult population.*[3]

With percentages like that for America's newest young adult generation, it is no wonder cultural secularism (atheism, agnosticism, or simply "who-cares-ism") is leaving a huge imprint on American morality (or the lack thereof). The sexual revolution of the '60s and '70s may have sown the wind, but without a doubt, we are now reaping the whirlwind of that sexual left turn. Today we inhabit an LGBTQ+ (an acronym for lesbian, gay, bisexual, transgender, and queer or questioning) culture that has pushed the limits of national morality to the place the United States Supreme Court has given its legal imprimatur in support of same-sex marriage, much to the consternation of evangelical Christian believers and activists.[4]

Then there is the Equality Act recently passed by the House of Representatives, considered by conservative Christian thought leaders as a dire warning of where this nation's collective morality may be headed, opening up yet another front in the culture wars of America. The Heritage Foundation summarized the bill this way:

> The proposed Equality Act of 2021 (H.R. 5) would make mainstream beliefs about marriage, biological facts about sex

differences, and many sincerely held beliefs punishable under the law. The Equality Act makes discrimination the law of the land by forcing Americans to conform to government-mandated beliefs under the threat of life-ruining financial and criminal penalties. Presented as a bill with commonsense and decent protections against discrimination, H.R. 5 is anything but. The Equality Act politicizes medicine and education and demolishes existing civil rights and constitutional freedoms.[5]

It is not my point here to argue the details of this congressional bill or plunge into the LGBTQ+ debate that rages elsewhere. But for thinking Americans, the seismic changes in our collective sexual mores are indicators of a national trend clearly moving away from historic biblical morality and values, a drift increasingly alarming to conservative evangelical Christians.

Nobody even argues it anymore: we are a nation divided to the core—politically, racially, sexually, morally, culturally, socially, economically, educationally, spiritually, religiously, demographically—fractured and poised on the edge of who knows what. At what point does the ominous warning of our Lord Jesus concern us? "If a kingdom [country] is divided against itself, that kingdom cannot stand. If a house [society] is divided against itself, that house cannot stand" (Mark 3:24, 25).

David French, in his new book, *Divided We Fall: America's Secession Threat and How to Restore Our Nation*, is blunt in his assessment: "It's time for Americans to wake up to a fundamental reality: The continued unity of the United States cannot be guaranteed. . . . There is not a single important cultural, religious, political or social force that is pulling Americans together more than it is pushing us apart."[6] What is he seeing that concerns him so?

> Nobody even argues it anymore: we are a nation divided to the core—politically, racially, sexually, morally, culturally, socially, economically, educationally, spiritually, religiously, demographically—fractured and poised on the edge of who knows what.

Americans are divided by their choices in news and popular culture. America remains the developing world's most religious nation, yet its increasingly secularized elites occupy one set of ZIP codes, while most traditional religious believers live in another. In politics, more and more Democrats are Democrats simply because they hate Republicans, and vice versa.

Ironically, cultural conservatives now find themselves hoping that the Supreme Court will protect them, said French, reached by telephone. Conservatives know they have lost Hollywood, academia, America's biggest corporations, the White House and both houses of Congress.

"I constructed the Texit scenario [French's hypothetical vision of how civil war could erupt again in this country] around court-packing, because that has become their [conservative's] last firewall," French said. "Remove that thin line of justices in black robes, and you open the door to what millions of Americans— especially religious conservatives—see as catastrophic changes . . . that could threaten our national unity."[7]

Interestingly enough, this "thin line of justices in black robes" who rule from the bench of the Supreme Court of the United States may be the last hope for some Americans—but may also become a growing concern for others. While not necessarily a bellwether for the future, the current composition of the Supreme Court—with six of its nine justices members of the Roman Catholic church—is a reminder that religious thought and loyalty are not negligible factors in legal interpretation, especially given Rome's expressed public commands to Catholic politicians (and jurists) to be faithful to church law, values, and polity.

The United States Conference of Catholic Bishops, in its statement "Catholics in Political Life," cautions: "The question has been raised as to whether the denial of Holy Communion to some Catholics in political life is necessary because of their public support for abortion on demand. Given the wide range of circumstances involved in arriving at a prudential judgment on a matter of this seriousness, we recognize that such decisions rest with the individual bishop in accord with the established canonical and pastoral principles."[8]

How Catholic politicians and jurists should understand that stance was evidenced by the statement made by Roman Catholic cardinal Raymond Burke during the recent presidential campaign:

> Cardinal Raymond Burke, a canon lawyer and formerly the prefect of the Church's highest court, has said that Catholic politicians supporting abortion should not receive Holy Communion, including pro-choice Catholic presidential candidate Joe Biden.
>
> Biden "is not a Catholic in good standing and he should not approach to receive Holy Communion," Burke said.[9]

Let there be no question about the ecclesiastical and personal influence bishops wield even in political debate. Should a matter of grave concern to Rome arise before the Supreme Court, it is not inconsequential that six of its nine justices, who ostensibly have pledged their fealty to their church, would be expected by Rome to support her stated doctrinal or moral agenda in the judicial-political arena of American life. Who can predict how this majority would rule?

On multiple fronts, it is increasingly evident America faces a critical moment in her once celebrated existence. If, as Jesus warned in Mark 3:25, "a house divided against itself" will collapse, it is not difficult to foresee how such a fall could, in fact, precipitate what we have examined in this book. Though at first it may have seemed improbable, if not impossible, the Apocalypse's prediction of an endgame coalition between the earth beast (America) and the sea beast (Rome) becomes much more likely in the context of a country bitterly divided and perhaps subsequently further weakened by some unnamed crisis (as we explored earlier).

Addressing the partisan divide among religious leaders, the syndicated columnist Michael Gerson wrote: "The moral convictions of many evangelical leaders have become a function of their partisan identification. . . . Blinded by political tribalism and hatred for their political opponents, these leaders can't see how they are undermining the causes to which they once dedicated their lives. Little remains of a distinctly Christian public witness."[10]

Given this void of spiritual or moral leadership, it is not hard to imagine Revelation's earth beast–sea beast confederacy stepping into that vacuum to legislate and enforce an act of national and eventually universal religious adherence. How would a country so deeply split on multiple levels ever find the voice to stand up to a national law commanding a universal day of worship, purportedly as an act of national unification?

All it would take is another crisis like the COVID-19 pandemic threatening the existential survival of America as we know it. Then would this nation's religious leaders, casting aside their fractious differences, hurriedly coalesce to call America back to God. "We have offended the Almighty, and His judgments will rain down until we return to Him." The message is easy to imagine, and the national response of contrition not hard to predict.

The prophetic scenario of Revelation 13, placed alongside the boiling-point instability and disunity of our society today, only adds fuel to the predictive warning: "When the state shall use its power to enforce the decrees and sustain the institutions of the church—then will Protestant America have formed an image to the papacy, and *there will be a national apostasy which will end only in national ruin.*"[11] The internet has become an echo chamber of diverse voices with their dire warnings of that ruin.

On multiple fronts, it is increasingly evident America faces a critical moment in her once celebrated existence. If, as Jesus warned in Mark 3:25, "a house divided against itself" will collapse, it is not difficult to foresee how such a fall could, in fact, precipitate what we have examined in this book.

Have we gone too far to avert this "national apostasy"? Is it too late to forestall this "national ruin"?

Not at all. But we can no longer call upon our political allegiances to save us or our country. Jen Pollock Michel is right:

> The kingdom of God is not painted in red or blue. Neither Republicans nor Democrats have their pulse on the kingdom of God, and for that matter the kingdom does not grow because of political influence and social clout. In fact, as Scripture makes clear, God's kingdom is frequently in conflict with the pharaohs and caesars of its day. Paradoxically, the kingdom of God seems to have all the vulnerability—and virulence—of a little seed. Even more surprising, the only way that this seed is ultimately harvested is through suffering. Unless a grain of wheat falls into the earth and dies, Jesus said.
>
> God's holy hill isn't Capitol Hill but Golgotha.[12]

And therein lies our help and our hope. The cry, "We have no king but Caesar" (John 19:15), must be met by the confession, "We have no King but Christ." "The Crucified One is the true king, the kingliest king of all; because it is he who is stretched on the cross, he turns an obscene instrument of torture into a throne of glory and 'reigns from the tree.' "[13]

And we who worship Christ as Lord and follow Him as King, "the kingliest king of all," are bound by those cords of allegiance to be unflinching in both loyalty and obedience to our Savior: "We must obey God rather than human beings" (Acts 5:29). So no matter what public opinion might eventually be, no matter how political parties might eventually align, no matter who national leaders might eventually become, the followers of Jesus have long known the truth:

> If any want to become my followers, let them deny themselves and take up their cross and follow me. For those who want to save their life will lose it, and those who lose their life for my sake, and for the sake of the gospel, will save it. For what will it profit them to gain the whole world and forfeit their life? Indeed, what can they give in return for their life? Those who are ashamed of me and of my words in this adulterous and sinful generation, of them the Son of Man will also be ashamed when he comes in the glory of his Father with the holy angels (Mark 8:34–38, NRSV).

Dietrich Bonhoeffer echoed Jesus' words with this immortalized summary, "When Christ calls a man, he bids him come and die."[14] Bonhoeffer's life as a pastor, writer, and theologian ended thus at age thirty-nine—hanged at the tethered end of a Nazi noose in the Flossenbürg concentration camp on April 9, 1945. But Jesus' words must not be taken to assure physical death when we take up the cross to follow Him: "It may be a death like that of the first disciples who had to leave home and work to follow him, or it may be a death like Luther's, who had to leave the monastery and go out into the world. But it is the same death every time—death in Jesus Christ . . . because only the man who is dead to his own will can follow Christ."[15]

It is no wonder in those dark years Bonhoeffer's "homilies and other church talks kept returning to the same profound question: What kind of theologian and pastor—*what kind of Christian*—must we encourage for the uncertain years ahead?"[16]

Given the uncertainty of the days before us these many years later, the question repeats itself: What kind of Christian, what kind of follower of Christ Jesus, who must take up our cross and follow Him, shall *we* be? "Come and die" is an invitation not lightly taken.

1. Shadi Hamid, "America Without God," *Atlantic*, published ahead of print, March 10, 2021, https://www.theatlantic.com/magazine/archive/2021/04/america-politics-religion/618072/.

2. James Emery White, *Meet Generation Z: Understanding and Reaching the New Post-Christian World* (Grand Rapids, MI: Baker Books, 2017), 37.

3. Barna, "Atheism Doubles Among Generation Z," January 24, 2018, https://www.barna.com/research/atheism-doubles-among-generation-z/; emphasis added.

4. *Christianity Today* introduced a series of articles on the subject: "Same-sex marriage has highlighted high-profile relationships between theology, church, state, and society. In June 2015 the Supreme Court issued its Obergefell v. Hodges decision, which ruled that states must allow same-sex couples to marry. A Pew Forum poll before the decision found that most Americans (57%) thought same-sex marriage should be legal, but less than a third of evangelicals agreed. Many are now asking questions about the difference between civil and religious marriage, the place of religious dissent on same-sex marriage, and pastoral care." "Same-Sex Marriage," *Christianity Today*, accessed June 13, 2021, https://www.christianitytoday.com/ct/topics/s/same-sex-marriage/.

5. "11 Myths about H.R. 5, the Equality Act of 2021," The Heritage Foundation, February 24, 2021, https://www.heritage.org/gender/report/11-myths-about-hr-5-the-equality-act-2021.

6. David French, *Divided We Fall: America's Secession Threat and How to Restore Our Nation* (New York: St. Martin's, 2020), 1.

7. Mattingly, "New Civil War?," https://www.arkansasonline.com/news/2021/jan/23/is-a-divided-nation-heading-for-a-new-civil-war/?features-religion.

8. "Catholics in Political Life," United States Conference of Catholic Bishops, accessed June 13, 2021, https://www.usccb.org/issues-and-action/faithful-citizenship/church-teaching/catholics-in-political-life.

9. CNA Staff, "Cardinal Burke: Biden Should Not Receive Holy Communion," Catholic News Agency, September 29, 2020, https://www.catholicnewsagency.com/news/cardinal-burke-biden-should-not-receive-holy-communion-15439.

10. Michael Gerson, "The Last Temptation," *Atlantic*, April 2018, https://www.theatlantic.com/magazine/archive/2018/04/the-last-temptation/554066/.

11. Ellen G. White, *Last Day Events* (Boise, ID: Pacific Press®, 1992), 134; emphasis added.

12. Jen Pollock Michel, *Surprised by Paradox: The Promise of And in an Either-Or World* (Downers Grove, IL: Intervarsity Press, 2019), 93.

13. F. F. Bruce, *The Gospel of John: Introduction, Exposition, and Notes* (Grand Rapids, MI: Eerdmans, 1983), 369.

14. Dietrich Bonhoeffer, *The Cost of Discipleship* (New York: MacMillan, 1974), 99.

15. Bonhoeffer, 99.

16. Charles Marsh, *Strange Glory: A Life of Dietrich Bonhoeffer* (New York: Alfred A. Knopf, 2014), 149.

"He has placed eternity in our hearts." Could it be we were made to live in another home somewhere else? Some pandemic-free, COVID-19–free, racial-fracture-free, poverty-and-politics-free, pain-and-perplexity-and-problem-free land . . . somewhere else?

FROM HERE TO ETERNITY

In the Bible, there is a line that goes something like this, speaking of God: "He has placed eternity in our hearts—in every human heart."[1] Atheist, agnostic, believer—it doesn't matter who you are—we were born with it, this piece of eternity embedded deep within our psyche.

In his book *The Journey of Desire: Searching for the Life We've Only Dreamed Of*, John Eldredge taps that embedded numinous sense of something more:

> "The heart," Blaise Pascal said, "has its reasons which reason knows not of." Something in us longs, hopes, maybe even at times believes that this is not the way things were supposed to be. Our desire fights the assault of death upon life. And so people with terminal illnesses get married. Prisoners in a concentration camp plant flowers. Lovers long-divorced still reach out in the night to embrace one who is no longer there. It's like the phantom pain experienced by those who have lost a limb. Feelings still emanate from that region where once was a crucial part of them, and they will sometimes find themselves being careful not to bang the corner of a table or slam the car door on a leg or an arm long since removed. Our hearts know similar reality. At some deep level, we refuse to accept the fact that this is the way things are, or must be, or always will be.[2]

"He has placed eternity in our hearts." Like phantom pain, we can feel it. G. K. Chesterton, in his book *Orthodoxy*, describes a change that came over him when as an agnostic, he came to believe in Christ as a very personal Being and Savior. Now, he writes, he could understand "why I could feel homesick at home."[3] Do you ever "feel homesick at home"?

"He has placed eternity in our hearts." Could it be we were made to live in another home somewhere else? Some pandemic-free, COVID-19–free, racial-fracture-free, poverty-and-politics-free, pain-and-perplexity-and-problem-free land . . . somewhere else? Could that be why, like Chesterton, we "feel homesick at home"?

"He has placed eternity in our hearts." It has been that way from the beginning of the pandemic of sin. Look at the ancients—they were just like we are.

> All these people were still living by faith when they died. They did not receive the things promised; they only saw them and welcomed them from a distance, admitting that they were foreigners and strangers on earth. People who say such things show that they are looking for a country of their own. If they had been thinking of the country they had left, they would have had opportunity to return. Instead, they were longing for a better country—a heavenly one. Therefore God is not ashamed to be called their God, for he has prepared a city for them (Hebrews 11:13–16).

No wonder they were "homesick at home." They, long before we, sensed this numinous, embedded, latent desire that something is missing, that "I'm not home yet."

Call it "hope" if you want—this "homesickness" that keeps driving us on. Ted Dekker, in his whimsical book, *The Slumber of Christianity: Awakening a Passion for Heaven on Earth*, captures the grip of hope or hopelessness that we all know only too well:

> What elevates our emotions, and what dashes them to the ground? What makes us jump for joy, and what sends us into a pit of deep discouragement?
>
> The answers are surprisingly simple: Hope. And hopelessness.[4]

Two competing, visceral emotions that have especially gripped society in this COVID-19 pandemic that doesn't seem to let go. Hope and hopelessness—we know them both, do we not?

Dekker goes on: "Hope is the primary force that drives human beings from hour to hour. Hope for a simple pleasure, a hug, a kiss, a juicy rib eye cooked to perfection. A new red Corvette, a beautiful home, a long vacation in Europe. The renewed health of an ill child or aging mother. These are among the many hopes that motivate our daily lives. Everything we do is driven by hope or hopelessness in one form or another."[5] He explains, "If you think about what changes your mood from one of happiness to one of sadness, you will always find hopelessness."[6]

There is more than enough hopelessness to go around these days. Have you noticed? Students and teachers unexpectedly banished from face-to-face learning to online teaching, only to return to the classrooms months later for in-person schooling. Then suddenly, both public and private sectors of education shift gears again into a new hybrid concoction of both remote and in-person teaching and learning. Will we ever return to normal? The back and forth of hopelessness. Businesses struggling to stay afloat in this "pandemicized" economy, "We're open" and then "We're closed," and then "Open" and eventually "Closed" again. And through it all, mortuaries, funeral homes, and cemeteries never go out of vogue, never are no longer needed.

How else shall we explain this "feeling homesick at home"? My wife, Karen, and I have spent some time with a homeless woman. All of her earthly belongings are packed into her small car—where she lives. She knows well the word *homeless*. And with all her heart she longs to not be homeless any longer. Maybe she is all of us—homeless and homesick while at home.

"He has placed eternity in our hearts." That gnawing homesickness that keeps whispering to us that we're not home yet.

Why, even the masses of those liberated slaves of Egypt, the children of Israel, were themselves driven by the promise of the Almighty that tapped deep into their sense of homesickness.

"And I [the God of your fathers and mothers] have promised to bring you up out of your misery in Egypt into a land . . . flowing with milk and honey" (Exodus 3:17). For forty subsequent long, wearying, dusty wilderness years, those delivered souls lived and longed for this "land flowing with milk and honey."

What's up with "milk and honey"? I'm not sure I would have survived forty years thinking of milk and honey. One commentator tries to help us out: "This was a proverbial expression for a land of plenty, and should not be pressed for a precisely literal meaning. It was intended as a figurative description of the great fertility and natural loveliness of the land of Canaan. Milk and honey are the simplest and choicest productions of a land abounding in grass and flowers, and were found in Palestine in great abundance."[7]

Twenty times in the Old Testament, God holds out this "milk and honey" enticement. A thousand years after the mighty Exodus, God is still holding out this "milk and honey" promise. Only now His children are in exile: "On that day I swore to them that I would bring them out of Egypt into a land I had searched out for them, a land flowing with milk and honey, the most beautiful of all lands" (Ezekiel 20:6).

There it is: "The most beautiful of all lands." Perhaps we think the same when we sing:

> America!
> America! God shed His grace on thee,
> And crown thy good with brotherhood
> From sea to shining sea.[8]

Turns out you can be in your own homeland and still "feel homesick at home." It could be your own homeland is far away—but like too many, you also can return home and still "feel homesick at home."

"He has placed eternity in our hearts."

How does that promise go? "Let not your heart be troubled; you believe in God, believe also in Me. In My Father's house are many mansions; if it were not so, I would have told you. I go to prepare a place for you. And if I go and prepare a place for you, I will come again and receive you to Myself; that where I am, there you may be also" (John 14:1–3, NKJV).

Homesick no longer! Did you ever hear or sing that old gospel song?

> I'm homesick for heaven, seems I cannot wait,
> Yearning to enter Zion's pearly gate;
> There, never a heartache, never a care,
> I long for my home over there.[9]

Jesus' promise is as good today as the night He made it: "I will come again, and receive you unto myself; that where I am, there ye may be also" (John 14:3, KJV).

Ever wonder what that home we are subconsciously homesick for is really like?

I read a piece in *Christianity Today* years ago that clicked with something I hadn't been able to express myself. Harry Blamires wrote in the essay:

> If only we could have the positives of earthly life without the

negatives. But that is precisely what heaven has to offer—the removal of the negatives. . . . [In heaven] both [human sin and the dominion of time] will be swept away. Here below, time withers flowers and human beauty, it encourages good intentions to evaporate, it deprives us of our loved ones. Within the universe ruled by time, the happiest marriage ends in death, the loveliest woman becomes a skeleton. Fading and aging, losing and failing, being deprived and being frustrated—these are negative aspects of life in time. Life in eternity will liberate us from all loss, all deprivation.[10]

Did you catch that? "That is precisely what heaven has to offer—the removal of the negatives." Isn't that the point Hebrews 11:16 is making? "They were longing for a better country—a heavenly one"—a country where all the negatives have been removed. No wonder these words are often read at funerals. Go ahead and count the seven negatives:

Then I saw "a new heaven and a new earth," for the first heaven and the first earth had passed away, and there was [1] no longer any sea. I saw the Holy City, the new Jerusalem, coming down out of heaven from God, prepared as a bride beautifully dressed for her husband. And I heard a loud voice from the throne saying, "Look! God's dwelling place is now among the people, and he will dwell with them. They will be his people, and God himself will be with them and be their God. '[2] He will wipe every tear from their eyes. There will be [3] no more death' or [4] mourning or [5] crying or [6] pain, for the [7] old order of things has passed away." He who was seated on the throne said, "I am making everything new!" Then he said, "Write this down, for these words are trustworthy and true" (Revelation 21:1–5).

> Turns out you can be in your own homeland and still "feel homesick at home." It could be your own homeland is far away—but like too many, you also can return home and still "feel homesick at home."

Did you notice them? Seven negatives, seven "no more of this" depictions. Blamires is right, "That is precisely what heaven has to offer—the removal of the negatives." Because that is the only way our human minds can comprehend heaven—to think of it without the negatives. That is, the "no mores" of the heartache of human existence will simply be no more: No more hospitals, no more divorce courts, no more prisons and jails and penitentiaries, no more food stamps, no more sleeping bags or garbage bags for the homeless. No more homelessness, nor more friendlessness, no more chemo, no more abuse, no more bankruptcies. No more anger, no more arguments, no more fighting, no more killing. No hatred or lying or cheating or losing or sinning.

The only way you and I can possibly imagine heaven is by "the removal of the negatives." Negatives obliterated, incinerated, and gone forever and ever. Amen.

But let's not end with the negatives (*what won't be there*). Why not end instead with the positives—*what will be there!* Here are seven of the great positives that will be there in heaven—each of them embedded in Scripture and annotated by a writer whose vision on occasion took in the glories of the Promised Land.

Positive no. 1—Jesus Himself will be there. What an appealing way to define heaven: "Heaven is where Christ is. Heaven would not be heaven to those who love Christ, if He were not there."[11]

How did Paul express it? "For to me, to live is Christ and to die is gain" (Philippians 1:21). Look, if Jesus is there, what else could matter? This same Jesus who will bear for eternity the ugly purple scars of His victory on the cross to save the likes of you and me. I am certain we will have occasion to clasp His nail-scarred hand in ours, and I imagine we will quietly weep. What else can gratitude say besides tears?

Positive no. 2—The Father Himself will be there. "The people of God are privileged to hold open communion with the Father and the Son. . . . We shall see Him face to face, without a dimming veil between. We shall stand in His presence and behold the glory of His countenance."[12]

We too often forget what Jesus told us: "Anyone who has seen me has seen the Father" (John 14:9). And a few minutes later, in that upper room the night before His death, Jesus assured us, "The Father himself loves you" (John 16:27). The truth is, no one has ever loved you more than your heavenly Father. You may never have been loved by your earthly father. But the day is coming when, at the feet of your heavenly Father, you will bask in a love so strong, so embracing, it will take your breath away. "And by [the Spirit] we cry, '*Abba* [the Aramaic child's word for Papa or Daddy], Father' " (Romans 8:15).

Positive no. 3—Our guardian angel will be there. Let your mind picture this moment: "Every redeemed one will understand the ministry of angels in his own life. The angel who was his guardian from his earliest moment; the angel who watched his steps, and covered his head in the day of peril; the angel who was with him in the valley of the shadow of death, who marked his resting place, who was the first to greet him in the resurrection morning—what will it be to hold converse with him, and to learn the history of divine interposition in the individual life, of heavenly co-operation in every work for humanity!"[13]

> The truth is, no one has ever loved you more than your heavenly Father. You may never have been loved by your earthly father. But the day is coming when, at the feet of your heavenly Father, you will bask in a love so strong, so embracing, it will take your breath away.

Describing us as children, Jesus once disclosed: "See that you do not despise one of these little ones. For I tell you that their angels in heaven always see the face of my Father in heaven" (Matthew 18:10). It turns out we all have our guardian angels: "The angel of the Lord encamps around those who fear him, and he delivers them" (Psalm 34:7).

Can you imagine the stories you and your guardian angel will share? "Say, Angel—do you remember that time I almost drowned?"

"Which one?"

"Up at the lake."

"Oh boy, do I remember! Who do you think kept you floating until I could get another human by your side?"

Then there are all those times you wept bitter tears: "Where, O where, is God when I so desperately need Him?" Turns out that unseen being, stationed at your side by Almighty God Himself, will rehearse to you the countless times he wept you through agonies—knowing your pain, holding you from hurting yourself.

Positive no. 4—God's friends through all history will be there.
"There the redeemed shall know, even as also they are known. . . . The pure communion with holy beings, the harmonious social life with the blessed angels and with the faithful ones of all ages who have washed their robes and made them white in the blood of the Lamb, the sacred ties that bind together 'the whole family in heaven and earth' (Ephesians 3:15)—these help to constitute the happiness of the redeemed."[14]

Who from sacred history would you like to sit down with for an all-afternoon visit? The firebrand Paul or the quiet and gentle John? Imagine the stories they will retell to you! Maybe it will be Ruth or Moses or Mary the mother of Jesus or David the forgiven king. What would an uninterrupted, deep conversation with these heroes of sacred history be like?

Or perhaps you would thrill to sit with the great reformer Martin Luther or the Baptist farmer-turned-revivalist William Miller. Talk about stories to share! Maybe science has been your intrigue, and an afternoon with Isaac Newton or perhaps (who am I to pronounce heaven's occupants?) even Albert Einstein would be the highlight of that week. Because there are more where these came from!

Positive no. 5—Heaven will be there.

> Language is altogether too feeble to attempt a description of heaven. As the scene rises before me, I am lost in amazement. Carried away with the surpassing splendor and excellent glory, I lay down the pen and exclaim, "Oh, what love! what wondrous love!" The most exalted language fails to describe the glory of heaven or the matchless depths of a Saviour's love. . . .
>
> If we could have but one view of the celestial city, we would never wish to dwell on earth again.[15]

So wrote Ellen White, who often described what she had witnessed above with such longing. In fact, there were times when, in a *Star-Trek*-on-steroids kind of moment, she was transported into the very glories of heaven, and on occasion she would beg not to be sent back to this darkened Earth. Why?

As it is written:

> "What no eye has seen,
>   what no ear has heard,

and what no human mind has conceived"—
the things God has prepared for those who love him—

these are the things God has revealed to us by his Spirit (1 Corinthians 2:9).

Positive no. 6—Advanced learning will be there. And for the university parish I pastor, this one has to be a must! "There, when the veil that darkens our vision shall be removed, and our eyes shall behold that world of beauty of which we now catch glimpses through the microscope; when we look on the glories of the heavens, now scanned afar through the telescope; when, the blight of sin removed, the whole earth shall appear in 'the beauty of the Lord our God,' what a field will be open to our study!"[16] But keep reading. "All the treasures of the universe will be open to the study of God's redeemed. Unfettered by mortality, they wing their tireless flights to worlds afar."[17]

There it is—proof we shall be students forever and ever, whether we ever attended a university or not.

Positive no. 7—The people we witnessed to will be there. "The redeemed will be sharers in His joy, as they behold, among the blessed, those who have been won to Christ through their prayers, their labors, and their loving sacrifice. As they gather about the great white throne, gladness unspeakable will fill their hearts, when they behold those whom they have won for Christ, and see that one has gained others, and these still others, all brought into the haven of rest, there to lay their crowns at Jesus' feet and praise Him through the endless cycles of eternity."[18]

I attended a friend's retirement party the other day, and the planners arranged for a group of singers to perform that Ray Boltz favorite "Thank You." The song is a story, a dream in which the songwriter and you, the listener, go to heaven together.

It is a touching song that chronicles a procession of individuals who come up to you in heaven and describe the difference your acts of kindness, your generosity, your volunteering service made in their lives. In fact, were it not for your demonstrated love for them, they would not be there with Jesus and you—that is the repeated underlying theme. And each encounter ends with Boltz's refrain:

Thank you for giving to the Lord
I am a life that was changed

Thank you for giving to the Lord
I am so glad you gave.[19]

Can you imagine the leaping joy in your heart over those thank-yous that will be expressed to you in heaven one day?

Here is the quotation we just read, now personalized for us: "Gladness unspeakable will fill [our] hearts, when [we] behold those whom [we] have won for Christ, and see that one has gained others, and these still others, all brought into the haven of rest, there to lay their crowns at Jesus' feet and praise Him through the endless cycles of eternity."[20] No wonder heaven will be such resplendent joy!

"He has placed eternity in our hearts." And that is why we must hold tightly to the hope we have: Hope that this, too, shall pass. Hope that Christ soon shall come. Hope that our family and our friends, our colleagues, and our neighbors will join us at His side. Hope that heaven will be our shared destiny and destination before too long.

And may I say, what a homecoming that will be!

Henry Gariepy in *100 Portraits of Christ* tells of Theodore Roosevelt, the former president of the United States, returning home from Africa after a grand hunting safari.

> As he boarded the ocean liner at that African port, crowds cheered his walk up the red carpet. He was feted with the finest suite aboard the ship. Stewards waited on him hand and foot during the transoceanic journey home. The former president was the center of the entire ship's attention.
>
> Also on board that vessel was another passenger, this one an elderly missionary who had given his life for God in Africa. His wife dead, his children gone, he now returned to his homeland alone. Not a soul on that ship noticed him.
>
> Upon the ocean liner's arrival at San Francisco, the president was given a hero's welcome with whistles blowing, bells ringing, and the awaiting crowd cheering as Roosevelt descended the gangplank in beaming glory.
>
> But there was nobody on hand to welcome the returning missionary. The elderly man found a small hotel for the night. As he knelt beside his bed, his heart broke: "Lord, I'm not complaining. But I don't understand. I gave my life for You in Africa. But it seems that no one cares. I just don't understand."

And then, in the darkness, it was as if God reached down from heaven and placed His hand upon the old man's shoulder and whispered, "Missionary, you're not home yet."[21]

In this season of the pandemic, with America's grip on the future tenuous at best, let us remind ourselves—we are not home yet. But there is a homecoming promised. And you have never seen a Welcome Home celebration like the one you are about to experience!

So please, remind the ones you love—we are not home yet.

Even so, come, Lord Jesus (Revelation 22:20, NKJV).

---

1. See Ecclesiastes 3:11.

2. John Eldredge, *The Journey of Desire: Searching for the Life We've Only Dreamed Of* (Nashville, TN: Thomas Nelson, 2000), 8.

3. G. K. Chesteron, *Orthodoxy* (Wheaton, IL: Harold Shaw, 1994), 83.

4. Ted Dekker, *The Slumber of Christianity: Awakening a Passion for Heaven on Earth* (Nashville, TN: Thomas Nelson, 2005), 34.

5. Dekker, 35.

6. Dekker, 34, 35.

7. *The Seventh-day Adventist Bible Commentary*, ed. Francis D. Nichol, vol. 1, *Genesis to Deuteronomy* (Washington, DC: Review and Herald, 1953), 510.

8. Katharine Lee Bates, "America the Beautiful" (1893).

9. Henry de Fluiter, "Homesick for Heaven" (1950).

10. Harry Blamires, "The Eternal Weight of Glory," *Christianity Today*, May 27, 1991, 30, https://www.christianitytoday.com/ct/1991/may-27/eternal-weight-of-glory.html.

11. Ellen G. White, *Last Day Events* (Boise, ID: Pacific Press®, 1992), 297.

12. Ellen G. White, *The Great Controversy* (Mountain View, CA: Pacific Press®, 1950), 676, 677.

13. Ellen G. White, *Education* (Oakland, CA: Pacific Press®, 1903), 305.

14. White, *Great Controversy*, 677.

15. White, *Last Day Events*, 287.

16. White, *Education*, 303.

17. White, *Great Controversy*, 677.

18. White, 647.

19. "Thank You for Giving to the Lord," Ray Boltz (Kobalt Music Publishing Ltd., Universal Music Publishing Group, 1988).

20. White, *Great Controversy*, 647.

21. Henry Gariepy, *100 Portraits of Christ* (n.p.: Cook Communications, 1993), 32, paraphrased.

It is my pastoral sense that the Spirit of God, who inspired the spirit of imminence in the New Testament, in fact, did intend for His message to be taken quite literally: "Live in daily expectation that Christ is coming soon—for your last breath is one breath away from your first breath at the return of Jesus."

EXCURSUS FROM FENWAY PARK:
YOU CAN GET THERE FROM HERE

Several years ago, I was asked if I believed Jesus is coming soon. Here is how I responded then. And frankly, it's how I still respond today.

> Having grown up a fifth-generation member of my Seventh-day Adventist faith community, it seems I have always lived with a sense that "Jesus is coming soon."
>
> And so, when asked today if I still believe in that imminence,[1] I choose to respond as the apostles did: "The end of all things is near" (1 Pet. 4:7); "The night is nearly over; the day is almost here" (Rom. 13:12); " 'In just a little while, he who is coming will come and will not delay' " (Heb. 10:37). Add to these confessions of imminence the declaration of our Lord Himself, woven into the Bible's last prayer, and what other stance is there for an Adventist (one who believes in the soon return of Christ) to embrace? " 'Yes, I am coming soon.' Amen. Come, Lord Jesus. The grace of the Lord Jesus be with God's people. Amen" (Rev. 22:20–21).
>
> Yes, but were those ancient texts ever intended to teach that Christ is returning *really* soon? Having officiated at the funerals of young men and women not even in their prime of life—cut down by the tragedy of an unexpected death—it is my pastoral sense that the Spirit of God, who inspired the spirit of imminence in the New Testament, in fact, did intend for His message to be taken quite literally: "Live in daily expectation that Christ is coming soon—for your last breath is one breath away from your first breath at the return of Jesus." [2]

But does that mean that Jesus could come in the lifetime of this third-millennial generation? But of course! The church isn't waiting on God—God is waiting on the church. But the moment you declare that conviction, a cry goes forth from friends, colleagues, and strangers alike, warning that such a notion somehow makes God dependent upon the church rather than the church dependent upon God. To which I offer this retort: nonsense! Reciprocal relationships have always been and always will be based upon mutual commitment to the relationship. How many couples have wisely put off their wedding day because one or both of them realized they were not yet ready for that "eternal" commitment? No more marriage then? Not at all—just more preparation and maturation before both are ready and both are eager for the big day.

The truth is God has been ready and eager since the last time-bound page was torn off the apocalyptic calendar.[3] His friend Ellen White reiterated that point with her handful of "the end could have come before this" statements. So then are we doomed to live out our days in some sort of eschatological limbo, never certain, never sure?

Chris Martenson, economic researcher and futurist, gives an example that has changed the way I think about the Second Coming.[4] Imagine, he says, that we're in Fenway Park, the stadium home of the Boston Red Sox. At noon, I handcuff you to the highest seat in the bleachers, and then with a magic eyedropper, I place a single drop of water on the pitcher's mound far below—a drop that magically doubles in size every minute. Imagine Fenway Park to be watertight, and your obvious assignment is to free yourself before the water level goes over your head. How much time do you have to break free of your handcuffs and get out of there before it's too late? The truth is, for minutes, you would see no appreciable increase in water—one drop becomes two, two drops become four, four drops become eight, and so on. In fact, at 12:44 P.M., there would only be 5 feet of water in the stadium. And that still leaves 93 percent of the stadium empty. But the startling reality is that if you do not extricate yourself within the next five minutes, your seat in the highest bleacher will be under water at 12:49 P.M. It is the power of compounding. For forty-four minutes, we think we have all the time in the world—but five minutes later, it's all over!

So it is, Martenson warns, with the planet today. He calls to mind graphs shaped like hockey sticks—global trends that for centuries have appeared to be flatlined with slow, incremental growth: Earth's population; oil, water, and food consumption; national debt; personal debt; and so on. To outward appearances, the stadium has hardly any water in it—plenty of time left to extricate ourselves. But as the researcher warns, in these opening years of the third millennium, Earth is facing a perfect storm of critical trends now simultaneously skyrocketing off the graphs: hemorrhaging debt (how many trillions of dollars has the US economy plunged further into debt just over this still-roiling pandemic?); oil and energy depletion; scarcity of water and food combined with a burgeoning number of mouths to feed. We thought we had time to get ready—but time's up.

Chris Martenson observes: "And that, right there, illustrates one of the key features of compound growth . . . the one thing I want you to take away from all this. *With exponential functions, the action really only heats up in the last few moments.*"[5]

In the last few moments? A century ago, the same point was made: "Great changes are soon to take place in our world, and the final movements will be rapid ones."[6] The apocalyptic focus of *The Great Controversy* concurs: "The end will come more quickly than [people] expect."[7] The point? While no one knows the date of Jesus' return, be forewarned the concept of an exponential function means that suddenly all the indicators will simultaneously spike—with blinding speed.

All it will take in this nation is a major crisis of crippling proportions—economic (a national financial collapse igniting urban violence and social meltdown), ecological (a killer quake, an errant asteroid leaving tens of thousands dead),[8] political (a terrorist's dirty bomb that destroys a city), military (a geopolitical misstep into World War III), and the list goes on. One major crisis and this nation will be on her knees, guided

> Earth is facing a "perfect storm" of critical trends now simultaneously skyrocketing off the graphs: hemorrhaging debt (how many trillions of dollars has the U.S. economy plunged further into debt just over this still roiling pandemic?); oil and energy depletion; scarcity of water and food combined with a burgeoning number of mouths to feed. We thought we had time to get ready—but time's up.

by the religious leaders of the land, pleading with God to withhold His judgments. Now factor in the social science research examined earlier in this book—that cataclysmic events create "conditions peculiarly fitted to the rapid alteration of belief systems"[9]—and it is not surprising that when faced with a choice between personal security and constitutional liberties, the majority will, as they did on the heels of the September 11, 2001, terrorist attacks, choose security first. Thus, crisis will become the catalyst hotbed that gives woeful birth to the apocalyptic endgame of Revelation outlined in this book. One crippling crisis is all it will take. Martenson's point—the last five minutes are critical.

Which is why we cannot afford the fatal delusion of the scoffers: "All things continue as they were from the beginning" (2 Peter 3:4, NKJV). No matter appearances, the last five minutes are critical.

So how then shall we live, standing as we are on the razor edge of eternity? Consider these seven provisions for endgame life:

1. "Grow in the grace and knowledge of our Lord and Savior Jesus Christ" (2 Peter 3:18)—so that we might flourish in our daily walk with God.
2. "How much more will your Father in heaven give the Holy Spirit to those who ask him" (Luke 11:13)—so that through His daily baptism we might be taught and empowered by the Spirit who knows Jesus best.[10]
3. "Go into all the world and preach the gospel to all creation" (Mark 16:15)—so that we might confidently share with the people around us the life and friendship we have found in our Savior.
4. "Whatever you [do] for one of the least of these brothers and sisters of mine, you [do] for me" (Matthew 25:40)—so that we might be both intentional and practical in giving compassion, assistance, companionship to those especially in need (emotionally or financially) during this pandemic and/economic downturn.
5. "May the God of hope fill you with all joy and peace as you trust in him, so that you may overflow with hope by the power of the Holy Spirit" (Romans 15:13)—so that we might be transformed into winsome, contagious disciples of Jesus.
6. "Being confident of this, that he who began a good work in you will carry it on to completion until the day of Christ Jesus" (Philippians 1:6)—so that we might not despair when we fall short, but rather rejoice over God's promise to finish in us what He has started—in time for Jesus' return.

7. "In this world you will have trouble. But take heart ['Be of good cheer' in NKJV]! I have overcome the world" (John 16:33)—so that, when all is said and done, we might go forth with confidence and joy, knowing that with Jesus, no matter the troubles that surround us now, the best is yet to come.

---

1. *Merriam-Webster* defines *imminence* as "the quality or state of being imminent [ready to take place, happening soon]." (*Merriam-Webster*, s.v. "imminence," accessed June 16, 2021, https://www.merriam-webster.com/dictionary/imminence.)

2. Dwight K. Nelson, "Five Minutes Later, It's Over!," *Adventist Review*, March 21, 2016, https://www.adventistreview.org/voices-dwight-k.-nelson.

3. See Daniel 8:14.

4. "Crash Course Chapter 4: Compounding Is the Problem," Peak Prosperity, accessed June 14, 2021, https://www.peakprosperity.com/video/crash-course-chapter-4-compounding -is-the-problem/.

5. "Crash Course;" emphasis added.

6. Ellen G. White, *Testimonies for the Church*, vol. 9 (Mountain View, CA: Pacific Press®, 1948), 11.

7. Ellen G. White, *The Great Controversy* (Mountain View, CA: Pacific Press®, 1950), 631.

8. See chapter 5, " 'Calamities Most Awful, Most Unexpected.' "

9. Michael Barkun, *Disaster and the Millenium*, reprint ed. (Syracuse, NY: Syracuse University Press, 1986), 6, quoted in Marvin Moore, *Could It Really Happen?* (Nampa, ID: Pacific Press®, 2007), 239.

10. The most profound and influential book I have ever read on the daily baptism of the Holy Spirit is Helmut Haubeil's *Steps to Personal Revival*. I urge you to download the ebook at no cost: https://steps-to-personal-revival.info. It is now available in more than forty-five languages. I pray the discovery you make through this book will change your life as it has mine.